Understanding Civilian Harm in Raqqa and Its Implications for Future Conflicts

MICHAEL J. MCNERNEY, GABRIELLE TARINI, NATE ROSENBLATT,
KAREN M. SUDKAMP, PAULINE MOORE, MICHELLE GRISÉ,
BENJAMIN J. SACKS, LARRY LEWIS

Prepared for the Office of the Secretary of Defense
Approved for public release; distribution unlimited

RAND NATIONAL DEFENSE RESEARCH INSTITUTE

For more information on this publication, visit **www.rand.org/t/RRA753-1**.

About RAND

Research Integrity

Published by the RAND Corporation, Santa Monica, Calif.

Library of Congress Cataloging-in-Publication Data is available for this publication.

ISBN: 978-1-9774-0694-1

Cover photo by Abood Hamam, used with permission.

Limited Print and Electronic Distribution Rights

About This Report

This report provides insights into the causes of civilian harm during the U.S.-led operation to liberate Raqqa, Syria, from the Islamic State of Iraq and Syria from June to October 2017. The purpose of the report is twofold: to help readers understand the causes of civilian harm in Raqqa and to help U.S. Department of Defense (DoD) policymakers and planners mitigate the risks of civilian harm in future conflicts.

Human Subject Protections (HSP) protocols were used in this study in accordance with the appropriate statutes and DoD regulations governing HSP. Additionally, the views of the sources rendered anonymous by HSP are solely their own and do not represent the official policy or position of DoD or the U.S. government.

National Security Research Division

The research reported here was completed in March 2021 and underwent security review with the sponsor and the Defense Office of Prepublication and Security Review before public release.

This research was sponsored by the Office of the Secretary of Defense and conducted within the International Security and Defense Policy Center of the RAND National Security Research Division (NSRD), which operates the RAND National Defense Research Institute (NDRI), a federally funded research and development center sponsored by the Office of the Secretary of Defense, the Joint Staff, the Unified Combatant Commands, the Navy, the Marine Corps, the defense agencies, and the defense intelligence enterprise.

For more information on the RAND International Security and Defense Policy Center, see www.rand.org/nsrd/isdp or contact the director (contact information is provided on the webpage).

Acknowledgments

We greatly appreciate the assistance provided by Deputy Assistant Secretary of Defense for Stability and Humanitarian Affairs Stephanie Hammond and her staff, particularly Cara Negrette, Anna Williams, and David Cate. We are also grateful to several people who provided us with assistance in our research efforts, including Loren Voss, Lt Col Breanna Fulton, Lt Col Mark Cramer, COL Daniel Gibson, Michael "Mick" Mulroy, and Eric Oehlerich. Thanks to Chris Woods from Airwars and Donatella Rovera from Amnesty International for sharing their insights and data. Thanks to Jenny McAvoy from InterAction for helping facilitate numerous fruitful discussions with nongovernmental organization officials.

We are indebted to our reviewers, Jeff Martini and Sarah Sewall, whose feedback improved this report tremendously. Brig Gen (retired) Matthew Isler's feedback was also crucial to our efforts.

We also recognize the invaluable contributions of the dozens of leaders and experts we interviewed from across the Department of Defense, Department of State, and many nongovernmental organizations.

Summary

The battle for Raqqa, Syria, seemed like a perfect storm of strategic and operational challenges. When the city was finally liberated from the Islamic State of Iraq and Syria (ISIS) in October 2017, 60 to 80 percent of it was estimated to be uninhabitable. In fact, the battle for Raqqa is a cautionary tale about civilian harm in 21st-century conflicts—perhaps like the hundred-year storm that arrives every decade, with characteristics that feel unique at the time but actually have been seen before and portend future trends. Many of the battle's lessons may apply to future urban combat situations, as well as conventional conflict scenarios more broadly. The purpose of this report is to discuss how the U.S. military—which is the best-trained and most technologically advanced military in the world, is supported in Operation Inherent Resolve by an international coalition of more than 80 countries, and was partnered in Raqqa with a well-respected militia force on the ground—could cause significant civilian harm despite a deeply ingrained commitment to the law of war.

Raqqa was not a unique case even at the time it occurred. Iraqi security forces, working with the U.S. military, caused more civilian casualties in their efforts to liberate Mosul from ISIS in 2016 and 2017, despite efforts to protect civilians. The Syrian regime of Bashar al-Assad, supported by Russian and Iranian partners, purposely targeted civilians and critical infrastructure in such cities as Aleppo to terrorize the population and force them to surrender. But Raqqa drew the attention of both U.S. Department of Defense (DoD) officials and nongovernmental organizations (NGOs) because the shocking level of destruction seemed so at odds with the pinpoint accuracy of many coalition air strikes, which provided the bulk of the firepower in the battle. What happened?

Although civilian harm is often equated with civilian casualties, it encompasses more than that. Civilian harm also includes displacement of populations and damage to structures and community infrastructure, such as bridges, hospitals, power sources, education and healthcare facilities, religious and cultural sites, and transportation hubs. Many of these locations support the health, safety, and well-being of the civilian population and receive special protections under the law of war. In the case of Raqqa, it is important to consider these broader elements of civilian harm and not limit analysis to the number of citizens killed or wounded in military operations.

The Office of the Secretary of Defense asked the RAND Corporation to study the causes of civilian harm in Raqqa, not only to understand what happened but also to provide insights into how DoD can reduce civilian harm in future operations. We collected data from a wide variety of sources, including DoD reports and guidance, military strike logs, analysis from NGOs, and interviews with more than 80 government and nongovernment officials and operators. This report primarily provides a U.S. perspective, and the bulk of the data analyzed came from U.S. government sources. Comprehensive data on the Raqqa operation were difficult to access even for those within DoD, and the utility of accessible data for quantitative analysis proved to be limited. We organized our research along three lines of effort, which are reflected in the structure of the report:

1. DoD's policies and procedures for mitigating civilian harm
2. the history of the battle for Raqqa, including a quantitative and qualitative analysis of the effects of the battle on civilians
3. the challenges of civilian harm mitigation in Raqqa through the lenses of ISIS tactics; U.S. airpower; U.S. ground units; U.S. partner forces (the Syrian Democratic Forces); U.S. intelligence; and U.S practices for identifying, assessing, and responding to civilian harm.

Although this study focuses on the battle to liberate Raqqa and the challenges that the U.S. military faced in mitigating civilian harm, it is important to start with the strategic context. First, the U.S. shift to a strategy of *encirclement* (surrounding ISIS and destroying it in the city) prior to the battle for Raqqa represented a more aggressive approach than the previous strategy of *attrition* (shoving ISIS from one position to another in Iraq and Syria). Second, the coalition's policy of focusing on operations in Iraq first meant that resources were prioritized for the Mosul operation, which ultimately limited the resources that were available for Raqqa, including those to analyze the civilian context of the battlespace. Third, Syria was in the midst of a civil war against a repressive central government that—along with its Russian and Iranian partners—took actions that increased civilian suffering in the country. This, combined with the challenges of supporting a Kurdish-led ground force to liberate an Arab city, made it particularly difficult for the coalition to understand the dynamics on the ground. Fourth, Turkey's geopolitical interests and redlines in Syria created challenges that significantly constrained the way in which coalition military options were conducted.

Thus, early strategic decisions of U.S. policymakers and some geopolitical constraints helped shape the hand that operational commanders were dealt. Military commanders faced other difficult challenges in the context of Raqqa: (1) a city of poorly constructed, multistory structures connected by secret tunnels and narrow alleys; (2) an enemy that was dug-in, capable, brutal, and desperate; (3) a coalition coordinating multiple countries and different U.S. military cultures (from the Air Force, special operations forces, and the Marine Corps); and (4) a less capable partner ground force with disparate Arab and Kurdish elements and few ties to the city it was trying to liberate. Finally, although the military adhered to the law of war, expectations about civilian casualty mitigation among both DoD and NGO officials had risen, given the technological and strategic superiority enjoyed by the U.S. military. But the civilian-harm challenges in conventional urban warfare are more complex than those that U.S. forces face in counterterrorism missions or even in counterinsurgency missions.

The Raqqa experience provides valuable insights into the challenges likely to characterize future combat with near-peer adversaries or competition with these adversaries through proxy military forces, and it raises the question of whether the United States and its allies are prepared to undertake the civilian protection responsibilities and meet the expectations that will accompany these future conflicts. We hope the findings and recommendations from this study can help our collective understanding of civilian harm in Raqqa and advance the U.S. approach to future conflicts.

Findings

From our research, we developed ten major findings.

U.S. Strategic Choices, Such as the Encirclement of Raqqa, Likely Increased Civilian Harm

Many of the circumstances around the battle for Raqqa—though perhaps unique in their details—portend the types of situations that are likely to arise again in the future: ruthless and committed adversaries, high-intensity urban combat environments, and complex geopolitical dilemmas. Specific U.S. policy choices, however, created some of the circumstances that were specific to Raqqa. These include, for example, the decisions to severely limit the number of U.S. ground forces, rely on less-capable partners, and prioritize operations in Iraq. Although we focused our study on operational challenges, we also analyzed the civilian-harm implications of one strategic choice in particular—the decision to encircle Raqqa—given the relevance it had for some of the operational challenges that followed.

The goal of shortening the length of the counter-ISIS campaign, and thereby potentially reducing overall levels of civilian harm, drove the shift "from shoving ISIS out of safe locations in an attrition fight to surrounding the enemy in their strongholds, so we can annihilate ISIS."[1] But this shift may have prevented the creation of civilian exit corridors and driven ISIS deeper into the densely-populated heart of the city. Pushing the adversary out of Raqqa and into terrain that was more sparsely populated would have allowed more fighters to escape and potentially lengthened the campaign. But the risk of civilian harm in Raqqa and other more heavily populated areas would clearly have been reduced.

The Coalition Made Considerable Efforts to Protect Civilian Life, but There Remains Room for Improvement

Nothing we present in this report should be interpreted as accusing coalition forces or leaders of violating the law of war. DoD abided by its policies and procedures, which go beyond the law of war, at multiple levels to help protect civilians during armed conflict.

Some military operators and commanders we interviewed identified opportunities to better integrate civilian-harm issues into the targeting cycle, and some leaders modeled the best practices that we discuss in our recommendations. In Raqqa, U.S. forces faced challenges using targeting tools to reduce civilian harm because of limitations on munitions and intelligence, surveillance, and reconnaissance (ISR); the prevalence of dynamic strikes; inconsistent use of assessments to enhance learning; and heavy reliance on a partner ground force.

Civilian Casualties in Raqqa Were Not as High as One Might Predict, Given the High Levels of Structural Damage

Civilians were trapped in a dense, urban conflict zone, and it was often extremely challenging for coalition forces to discern civilian presence. However, the high levels of structural damage in Raqqa should have implied a higher civilian casualty rate, if circumstances in Mosul and Aleppo were any indication. In Mosul and Aleppo, there was one building damaged per civilian casualty; in Raqqa, the ratio of structures damaged to civilian casualties was about three to one.

---

[1] Jim Garamone, "Mattis, Dunford, McGurk Cite Coalition Progress to Annihilate ISIS," U.S. Department of Defense, May 19, 2017a; and DoD-hosted civilian casualties roundtable discussion with NGO officials, March 2020.

In addition, the rate of civilian casualty incidents in Raqqa was lower than what might otherwise be expected, given the rate of fires during the operation. Several factors may have contributed to these outcomes. The first factor is the shrinking size of the battlespace in Raqqa. As the rate of munitions employed in the Raqqa operation rose in late August 2017, the number of civilian casualty incidents reported declined until nearly the end of the operation. One reason for this gap may be that ISIS controlled fewer neighborhoods in Raqqa by September 2017, and therefore fewer civilians could be put in harm's way. Second, the steady decline of civilians remaining in Raqqa during the operation indicates that it was possible, albeit difficult, for civilians to leave Raqqa, despite the coalition's overall strategy for encircling and destroying ISIS in Raqqa.

ISIS's Defensive Tactics Deliberately Put Civilians in Harm's Way

ISIS snipers were dispersed throughout the city to shoot fleeing civilians. ISIS also embedded suicide bombers to blow themselves up in groups of civilians who tried to leave. Fighters forcibly relocated civilians to areas near their front lines as the coalition offensive progressed, and the fighters rigged buildings with explosives to cause civilian harm that they could then blame on coalition air strikes. Many civilian deaths in Raqqa occurred as a direct result of ISIS actions.

Extensive Structural Damage in Raqqa Undermined Post-Battle Governing Prospects and Long-Term U.S. Interests

Although coalition forces focused intently on the civilian casualty risk for each strike, they largely ignored the impact of their actions on civilian livelihoods over the long term. As a result, Raqqa endured the most structural damage by density of any city in Syria. This reality, plus the lack of U.S. support or planning for Raqqa's reconstruction, impeded CJTF-OIR's intention to return Raqqa to local governance and thereby help protect the city from ISIS's re-emergence.

Airpower Was Not Used to Shape the Battlefield in Raqqa, Which Made Civilian-Harm Mitigation More Difficult

Pre-offensive operations to shape the battlefield in ways that would reduce the risks of civilian harm were insufficient. Moreover, shaping operations (i.e., striking ISIS targets behind front lines) stopped once the battle transitioned from isolating the city to seizing it. The practical effect of this approach was that nearly all strikes in Raqqa were dynamic, and it took more dynamic strikes to get through the city.

The primary limitation of shaping during the seizure of Raqqa was that the coalition lacked an operational-level headquarters for the Raqqa operation to lead deliberate targeting efforts and lacked teams resourced to conduct the intelligence fusion needed for targeting.

Air operators made important adaptations over the course of the campaign. These adaptations included loading fighter jets with a variety of explosive yields, fusing options, and guidance mechanisms. This helped ensure that pilots were able to choose appropriate weapons for individual air strikes, minimizing the flight time of a weapon so that ISIS fighters would not have the chance to walk into an area where civilians were present. Adjusting fusing timers could help minimize the amount of fragmentation of the bomb while still meeting the commander's intent for the strike. Increased joint planning and mission rehearsals between air and ground operators may have allowed adaptations like these to take effect earlier in the campaign.

Restrictions on U.S. Ground Forces Made Preventing Civilian Harm More Difficult

U.S. forces faced a considerable risk trade-off in conducting what was primarily an air campaign against ISIS in Raqqa and relying only on a limited ground presence. Having more ground forces, specifically infantry units, could have improved U.S. and coalition capabilities to mitigate and respond to civilian harm through interactions with the local population inside Raqqa. A larger ground troop presence also could have provided a direct link between the battlefield and pilots dropping munitions, conducted targeted raids on buildings housing ISIS snipers, and initiated the civilian casualty response process in the case of unintended incidents of harm. Instead, the United States and its coalition partners prioritized airpower to reduce risk to their own forces on the battlefield, a move that inhibited information collection and vetting, curtailed knowledge of the civilian environment inside Raqqa, and made it more difficult to discern noncombatants from combatants. As a result, precision targeting was especially difficult for artillery units situated outside the city. Ultimately, shifting to an air campaign in an effort to reduce the potential for U.S. and coalition casualties displaced significant risk onto Raqqa's civilian population and jeopardized strategic objectives.

Restrictive authorities over sustained information operations also hindered the ability of ground forces to shape the environment in a way that could help protect remaining civilians. Our research also suggests that operating as a joint force posed some challenges to U.S. ground forces as they worked to mitigate civilian harm. In particular, the different services sometimes adhered to different operational cultures, and the frequent rotation of conventional ground forces caused some messaging and best practices to become lost as units moved in and out of the area.

Irregular Partner Forces Were Less Precise Than U.S. Forces Would Be and Increased the Risk of Civilian Harm

There were two major categories of civilian harm risk in Raqqa. First was the risk of civilian harm posed by the operations of the Syrian Democratic Forces (SDF). The SDF took steps to protect civilians before and during the battle for Raqqa; however, to preserve its limited forces, the SDF likely risked greater civilian harm than a comparable U.S. force would have. The SDF was also insufficiently trained on civilian-harm mitigation. Beyond providing a one-hour training session on the law of war, the coalition did not systematically work with the SDF to impart policies and practices on mitigating civilian harm. The U.S. Department of State, international organizations, NGOs, and other key players were not consulted.

The second category of civilian-harm risk was that caused by U.S. and coalition forces while providing support to the SDF. First, U.S. forces did not have command and control over SDF fighters, which put the United States in the position of having to help or sometimes rescue its partners when they got themselves into dangerous situations. Second, without heavy weapons of their own, the SDF required substantial support from coalition fires, leading to greater destruction. Strikes that are launched to defend a partner (called *self-defense strikes*) increase the risk of civilian harm because of the compressed timeline in which they occur, the lack of U.S. joint terminal attack controllers on the front lines to provide precise close air support, and potential difficulties verifying partner targets with limited ISR assets.

A Lack of Sources to Provide Better Local Information Impeded Civilian-Harm Mitigation Efforts

The lack of U.S. ground forces in Raqqa, as described earlier, exacerbated the need for other sources of intelligence, including human intelligence, open-source intelligence, and other forms of publicly available information; these were all lacking. Instead, the intelligence collection apparatus was biased from the top down, relying primarily on air sensors and strategic ISR assets. Human intelligence encourages a ground-up understanding of the environment, including the human terrain, which can reduce potential target misidentification issues or a bias of assuming guilt until innocence is proven.

Rather than redouble efforts to overcome ISIS's suppression of human sources on the ground, coalition leaders took the more traditional intelligence collection approach of focusing on the end state of the military operation—that is, defeating the enemy—and put insufficient emphasis on finding ways to understand the human terrain and mitigate civilian-harm risks.

Flawed DoD Processes and Poor Collection of Civilian Casualty Data Hindered the Military's Ability to Assess and Analyze Civilian Harm in Raqqa

In Raqqa, the detection of civilian casualties by the U.S. military relied largely on military operational data and air-based assets to determine whether and how much civilian harm occurred after a strike. Through this study, we found that both of these sources of data had critical flaws, which prevented the military from recording a comprehensive assessment of civilian harm in the aftermath of the Raqqa operation.

Without reliable operational data, it is impossible for the military to understand the root causes of civilian casualties, characterize patterns of harm, and identify specific measures that U.S. forces can take to mitigate civilian harm while preserving mission effectiveness and force protection.

Recommendations for Future Improvements

Our findings demonstrate that mitigating and responding to civilian harm are not just operational issues that fall exclusively on the shoulders of commanders and operators on the battlefield. Instead, they are issues that cut across the military as an institution and that should be addressed in decisions related to manning, training, and equipping the entire force; in the joint planning process; and from an operational perspective. Each of these elements provides opportunities to derive best practices around civilian harm so that they become institutionalized across DoD. From our research, we developed eight categories of recommendations that reflect this overarching finding.

Prior to the Start of Military Operations, DoD Must Take a Broader Approach to Civilian Harm That Considers How Strategic Choices Might Affect Civilian-Harm Risks

- Improved operational design can better account for civilian protection during the predicted flow of a battle and for the long-term welfare of the civilian population. A broader approach to civilian harm should consider the implications of strategic choices, such as the number of U.S. ground forces, restrictions on U.S. ground forces, air and intelligence resources committed to the operation, reliance on partners, attrition versus encirclement strategies, preservation of infrastructure, and other longer-term considerations.

- To avoid alienating the very population that has been liberated, as happened in Raqqa, strategy development should better account for efforts to remove explosive hazards, reestablish essential services, and secure an area so that civilians can move back into their communities quickly and safely, ultimately empowering them to rebuild their city. For example, if military commanders express preservation of infrastructure in their intent, then staffs and targeting planners will execute that intent. Policymakers must also express this intent and ensure that resources flow to that objective, even after military objectives have been achieved.
- U.S. forces should more intensively engage NGO staffs as part of their planning, operations, and post-battle assessments.
- Future planning would benefit from more-intensive risk-benefit analysis of confronting enemies in various environments (e.g., urban versus rural) and involving various types of partners and various levels of U.S. and coalition air and ground forces.
- Officials from the Office of the Secretary of Defense, the Joint Staff, and combatant commands should consider ways to use table-top exercises, wargaming, and modeling and simulation tools to better understand the implications of their strategies through a civilian-harm lens. For example, wargames might ask participants to assess whether a certain scenario presents joint forces with the opportunity to push or incentivize an enemy out of urban areas prior to encirclement, despite obvious risks.

DoD Can Improve Its Application of Targeting Processes, Targeting Tools, and Force Preparation

- Guidance at every level (coalition, Office of the Secretary of Defense, Joint Staff, military service, combatant command, and task force) should direct that policymakers and military leaders consider resource requirements, including ISR and munitions with low collateral damage, from the perspective of civilian-harm mitigation.
- DoD doctrine and training should emphasize that leaders use every formal and informal means of providing guidance—including planning documents, expressions of commander's intent, and face-to-face discussions—to emphasize the importance of mitigating civilian harm.
- Professional military education and training components should consistently emphasize civilian-harm assessments as learning tools, work to share lessons among units, and institutionalize those lessons for future learning.

DoD Should Harness the Considerable Lessons Learned from Raqqa—and from Past Operations—to Better Prepare Ground Forces, Pilots, and Targeting Teams for Future Urban Engagements, Partly Through Improved Education and Training

- Prioritizing civilian-harm mitigation through battlefield-shaping operations using air and ground assets may reduce reliance on dynamic (including self-defense) strikes, which typically carry greater risk to civilians.
- Planners and operators should consider developing compressed-timeline methods for estimating collateral damage and improved tools for understanding the operating environment during dynamic or defensive strikes.

- Professional military education for officers who will operate in the joint environment—including graduate school programs, such as the Army's School of Advanced Military Studies and the Air Force's School of Advanced Air and Space Studies—should directly integrate training around the complexities of mitigating and responding to civilian harm. Applying such techniques as wargames and exercises involving repetitions to develop deeper insights into civilian-harm risks would greatly benefit leaders preparing to operate in a joint environment.
- Pre-deployment training cycles should build in practical evolutions that expose air and ground force planners and operators to the complexities that they are likely to face on the battlefield when it comes to mitigating civilian harm. Training is likely to be most effective if it is led by military personnel with personal experience dealing with such issues in a joint environment (as planners and operators) and if it employs vignettes and tactical decision games from recent operations. Large-scale strategic and planning-level exercises, for instance, could force planners and operators to make complex decisions similar to those made in the Raqqa context—for example, about the appropriate supply of various types of munitions carried by pilots or about whether to launch suppressive fires in support of partner forces in dense urban environments.
- Urban warfare is likely to characterize future conflicts, and ground units must be better trained to operate in such environments in a way that mitigates civilian harm. In particular, professional military education for officers who will operate in the joint environment should regularly integrate instruction around the complexities of mitigating and responding to civilian harm and should adapt and update instructional modules to ensure that they draw on recent and relevant combat experiences. Pre-deployment training cycles should enhance existing law of war and ROE training by building in practical evolutions that expose ground force operators to the complexities that they are likely to face on the battlefield when it comes to mitigating civilian harm.

Although our analysis of the air and ground components of the anti-ISIS campaign in Raqqa led us to these recommendations, they apply to multiple segments of the U.S. military joint force.

An Increased Emphasis on Information Operations Could Reduce Civilian-Harm Risk

- U.S. military planners should prioritize information operations, including broadly disseminating messaging that emphasizes the enemy's use of tactics that violate the law of war. Through targeted information campaigns, U.S. forces can play a larger role in delegitimizing enemy forces, particularly those that share few, if any, ties to local populations and suffer from a lack of popular support. There is a role here for ground planners and operators, as well as for public affairs officers who can broadly disseminate messaging about enemy tactics across a variety of communication platforms.
- Although U.S. forces made some efforts in the lead-up to the Raqqa campaign to communicate with local civilians, more-concerted and widely applied strategies to disseminate information and shape the overarching narrative could go a long way to mitigate civilian harm. The joint force should consider delegating authority over information operations to lower levels—for example, to battalion or squadron commanders—to effectively layer information operations into existing civilian-harm mitigation policies.

Partnering Efforts Between the United States and Local Forces Should Prioritize Strategies and Tactics to Mitigate Civilian Harm During Military Operations

There are four principal ways in which the United States could help mitigate civilian harm in its partnerships:

- At the start of a partnership, DoD officials, in consultation with the Department of State, should assess a local force's capacity and will to mitigate civilian harm.
- Using the results of that assessment, the United States should take tailored steps prior to the operation to build a partner's capacity and capability on civilian-harm issues. Training on civilian-harm mitigation practices is an important part of this capacity-building and should be crafted in consultation with the Department of State.
- Throughout an operation, DoD should plan to tailor its operational support to address a partner's risks and leverage its strengths. Such operational support to partners might include assisting with collateral damage estimation, leveraging U.S. ISR assets to help a partner with targeting, and providing partners with weapons that are effective in close combat situations to avoid air strikes on buildings.
- DoD should collect information regarding instances of civilian harm caused by partner forces to avoid accountability gaps. Where feasible, the military should also consider establishing a process for how to use partner, U.S. government, and publicly available sources to gather information on how U.S. equipment and weapons are used by partners operationally.

The U.S. Military and Intelligence Community Should Investigate Opportunities to Develop Tools and Practices That Improve Understanding of the Civilian Environment and Better Leverage Open-Source Intelligence, Publicly Available Information, and Human Intelligence

- To further bolster the effort to improve inputs into target-development processes, we recommend developing intelligence-specific tradecraft and training to support improved human terrain analysis, efforts to validate open-source information, improved civilian casualty assessments, and any associated requirements for collecting open-source intelligence and publicly available information.
- Combatant commands, in concert with U.S. intelligence agencies, should explore ways to dynamically incorporate open-source intelligence and publicly available information into applications to provide a common operational picture that incorporates this information. With smartphones and social media, every person becomes a potential sensor who collects valuable information about their environment, and this information can be leveraged into open-source intelligence. This may become increasingly challenging with the continued move to remote operations that rely on air assets and even remotely controlled assets, but it is critical to ensuring a necessary level of understanding of the civilian environment. Office of the Secretary of Defense and military service staff should support these requirements through the development of improved technical capabilities.

DoD Must Take Several Steps to Improve Its Ability to Assess and Investigate Civilian Harm, Including Improving Collection and Analysis of Civilian Casualty Data, Simplifying Reporting Procedures and Making Them Consistent, and Establishing Criteria for When the Military Should Conduct Site Visits

- The U.S. military should improve its data collection methods, including storage of and access to strike data, in a single program to enable more-accurate tracking and recording of civilian-harm incidents.
- DoD should simplify and streamline its reporting procedures and help local residents, NGOs, and international organizations better report civilian casualty incidents. For NGOs and international organizations, DoD should provide a better understanding of the civilian casualty cells, what information is needed, and how it should be received.
- Collecting and storing high-quality data on civilian casualties does not have to be a burden imposed on the commands. We found that detailed post-operation analysis of the relationship between strikes and civilian casualties can help improve targeting, reduce civilian casualties, and support achieving mission objectives in the future.
- DoD should establish clearer criteria for when the military should conduct site visits. One of the primary purposes for a site visit is typically to assess causation—whether or not a U.S. military action was the cause of the reported civilian casualties. Proving this hypothesis, true or false, might require gathering forensic evidence to improve the military's understanding of the structure and mode of failure, as well as the terrain.

DoD Must Go Beyond the Identification of Lessons Regarding Civilian Harm—Exemplified in This Study but Also in Past Studies on Civilian Harm—and Ensure That They Are Acted On

- DoD's weak institutional learning for civilian-harm issues meant that past lessons went unheeded, increasing the risk to civilians in Raqqa. Although the combination of the nuances of the operating environment, the nature of the threat, the complications of working with a less proficient partner, and leadership pressure to end the conflict rapidly created a perfect storm for civilian harm, many of the factors contributing to such harm in Raqqa had been observed before. In our research, we uncovered past DoD lessons regarding civilian harm that were not incorporated into DoD practices and did not inform operations in Raqqa. Without a strengthened learning process, there is a real risk that the tragic circumstances seen in Raqqa will be repeated.
- This lack of historical progress is likely a result of several factors: a lack of needed consistent attention from DoD leadership, under-resourcing of efforts to clearly identify lessons during and after operations, and unclear responsibilities for ensuring that institutional changes are made. These responsibilities need to be clearly established, properly resourced, and sustained in order for DoD to improve over time.

Contents

Figures and Tables

Figures

Tables

CHAPTER ONE

Introduction

Azad was stressed. He and his small Kurdish unit were pinned down. They hoped it was just a single sniper on the third floor of the building across the courtyard. But the day before, it was a handful of foreign fighters with AK-47s, rocket-propelled grenades, and a heavy machine gun. And improvised explosive devices, of course. They were everywhere. Azad lost three men the previous day; he could not afford to lose more. "Why are we getting killed to liberate an Arab city from a bunch of terrorists?" asked one of his men the night before. "We will not be safe until Daesh is annihilated," Azad had responded. "You want to negotiate with these men who wear suicide vests, who torture captives and enslave girls?"

An explosion knocked Azad forward. Now someone was firing rockets into their position, and someone else had started shooting at them. The rounds seemed to be coming from the same building. Azad pulled out the tablet given to him by his U.S. advisers, called back to Sergeant Tom, and requested an air strike. "I've got five or six Daesh, sniper fire, AK-47s, RPGs." The sergeant, who could track Azad's location using the tablet, asked, "You got eyes on?" "Yes, hurry," Azad said and provided the coordinates.

Master Sergeant Tom Harvey cross-checked the information and called back to the coalition strike cell for close air support. He was only a couple of miles away from Azad, but it felt like he was in Timbuktu at this moment. Azad and his lightly armed fighters were brave and devoted to their U.S. special forces advisers, but the Americans were not allowed to accompany them to the front lines of the fighting. Azad's unit had taken heavy losses over the past few weeks and could not afford many more. The neighborhood where they were fighting had tall buildings and narrow alleys draped in tarps by the enemy to obstruct the views from above. The strike cell relied on the Combined Air Operations Center at Al Udeid Air Base in Qatar to ensure that the right planes with the right munitions were available. It was a challenge with the big fight in Mosul, Iraq, going on simultaneously to this fight in Raqqa, Syria. "The Combined Air Operations Center provides the menu, and the strike cell chooses the entrée," Tom liked to say.

Despite the challenges, the process was clear and often had borderline-miraculous results. Skilled pilots could maneuver over an alley and fire into a single window, killing the fighters inside while leaving the rest of the building intact. Pilots could delay the explosion of weapons by 60 milliseconds to spare friendly forces and civilians from bomb fragmentation. Every once in a while, though, a target was particularly hard to pinpoint, the ideal angle was not possible to achieve, the ideal aircraft or munition was not available, or an entire building was nominated as a target. But, in this instance, Tom's friend Azad and fighters like him were under attack by six enemy fighters. Or maybe it was four or two. Or maybe it was 12 fighters moving around a booby-trapped building, ready to wipe out Azad's team if they stormed inside. Maybe, despite intelligence reporting, satellite imagery, and hundreds of hours of full-motion video surveillance, there were unseen civilians huddled in the basement of this building. Maybe the enemy had rigged the building with explosives so that it would collapse on top of these civilians when a guided missile struck the single fighter who remained after his comrades slipped through a tunnel to another building.

* * * *

Despite having the world's greatest technology and training, the U.S. military is still subject to the fog of war and to political and resource constraints. The fictional story of Azad, a member of the Syrian Democratic Forces (SDF), and Sergeant Tom, a U.S. special operator, reflects hundreds of real-life stories that took place in Raqqa in 2017. The battle for Raqqa was a perfect storm of geopolitical, operational, and tactical challenges and choices. The level of destruction and civilian harm in Raqqa were high enough to draw the attention not only of humanitarian organizations but also of U.S. military operators and senior defense officials. Several reports have documented the perspectives of civilians harmed by military operations in Raqqa; all are important for documenting and drawing attention to the human costs of war.[1]

We hope that this report complements those efforts by providing a U.S. strategic and operational perspective of the battle for Raqqa in order to help U.S. Department of Defense (DoD) personnel and others across the U.S. government improve their ability to mitigate civilian harm in future operations.

Raqqa as a Strategic Perfect Storm for Civilian-Harm Risk

The battle for Raqqa was an important milestone for Operation Inherent Resolve (OIR), the military campaign against the Islamic State of Iraq and Syria (ISIS), which involves a U.S.-led coalition of more than 80 members.[2] Raqqa was the last major ISIS-held city in Syria and the administrative capital of ISIS's self-proclaimed caliphate. As *Time* magazine reported after the battle, "With the fall of Raqqa, this idea of a caliphate is at an end. No longer in control of any major city in Iraq or Syria, ISIS is on the verge of defeat as a conventional military force."[3]

OIR has been a difficult campaign from its initial air strikes in 2014 to the fall of ISIS's last stronghold in Baghouz, Syria, in March 2019 and beyond. As we will describe in this report, U.S. military forces took important steps to mitigate the risks of civilian harm but were also underprepared for the operational challenges of Raqqa and could have performed better in mitigating civilian-harm risk, despite past efforts to document hard-earned lessons from other operations.[4] In this report, we define *civilian harm* broadly to include damage, injury, or death that adversely affects civilian populations, structures, or infrastructure as a consequence of military operations. This is not to imply that a building is as important as a human life but

---

[1] See, for example, Amnesty International, *"War of Annihilation": Devastating Toll on Civilians, Raqqa – Syria*, London, 2018.

[2] ISIS is also called Daesh, the Islamic State, and the Islamic State of Iraq and the Levant.

[3] Jared Malsin, "Raqqa Is in Ruins, and ISIS in Retreat," *Time*, November 6, 2017.

[4] For a detailed analysis of the institutional incorporation of lessons learned on this topic, see Sarah B. Sewall, *Chasing Success: Air Force Efforts to Reduce Civilian Harm*, Maxwell Air Force Base, Ala.: Air Force University Press, 2016.

rather to highlight the fact that military operations cause harm that affects civilian populations long after the fighting stops.

The bulk of our research focused on operational challenges and how U.S. military forces can continue to improve. But there were other factors above and beyond the operational level that created a strategic perfect storm, constraining operational forces in ways that may have seemed uniquely problematic at the time yet provide important lessons for future conflicts. As we discuss in Chapter Five, some of these factors related to an enemy that not only violated the law of war but also exploited U.S. adherence to it, creating dilemmas that U.S. forces and policymakers should expect from other adversaries. Other factors were related to U.S. policy decisions and geopolitical constraints. These choices and constraints made it more difficult for military operators to mitigate civilian harm, and although our research does not evaluate every factor in depth, we provide some strategic context by highlighting four of them here.

First, just days before the start of the Raqqa campaign in May 2017, U.S. Secretary of Defense James Mattis announced that President Donald Trump "directed a tactical shift from shoving ISIS out of safe locations in an attrition fight to surrounding the enemy in their strongholds so we can annihilate ISIS."[5] Both the *attrition* and *encirclement* approaches created challenges for military planners constrained by a small U.S. footprint and working through a nonstate partner force on the ground in Syria. Attrition, executed through local partner forces, had potentially worked to prolong the conflict, as ISIS fighters slipped away from each battle to live and fight another day in Iraq and Syria. One DoD official whom we interviewed noted that, as part of the attrition strategy, the SDF became adept at the "pincer movement," in which partner forces attacked ISIS on two flanks, which allowed civilians (but also ISIS fighters) to flee out the back.[6] There was a deliberate decision to abandon this approach in Raqqa in favor of encirclement in order to prevent ISIS fighters from escaping the battlefield, instead forcing them to fight the battle in the city.[7] This decision was driven in large part by terrorist attacks in Europe by ISIS or ISIS-inspired foreign fighters. Encirclement presented a more aggressive approach: Although there were arguments for dedicating greater U.S. resources to the defeat and stabilization of Raqqa, including a commitment of U.S. and coalition ground forces, this was not the choice that policymakers ultimately made.[8]

Second, simultaneous operations in Mosul, Iraq, and other DoD requirements around the world strained the system responsible for providing the necessary intelligence, surveillance, and reconnaissance (ISR) support crucial to both the effective targeting of ISIS and the mitigation and assessment of civilian harm. Combined Joint Task Force (CJTF)-OIR had a policy of focusing on operations in Iraq first and thus prioritized U.S. and coalition resources for the

---

[5] Ellen Mitchell, "Mattis: Trump Strategy Aims to 'Annihilate' ISIS," *The Hill*, May 19, 2017. See also Jim Garamone, "Defeat ISIS 'Annihilation' Campaign Accelerating, Mattis Says," U.S. Department of Defense, May 28, 2017b.

[6] Senior DoD official, interview with the authors, March 2020.

[7] Senior DoD official, interview with the authors, March 2020.

[8] Seth G. Jones, James Dobbins, Daniel Byman, Christopher S. Chivvis, Ben Connable, Jeffrey Martini, Eric Robinson, and Nathan Chandler, *Rolling Back the Islamic State*, Santa Monica, Calif.: RAND Corporation, RR-1912, 2017, pp. 93–106.

Mosul operation, which ultimately limited the resources available to analyze the human terrain[9] and shape the battlespace in Raqqa.[10]

Third, Syria lacked a central government that could, in theory, take responsibility for balancing the risks to civilians against the need to destroy ISIS. An international coalition working "by, with, and through" a Kurdish-led ground force to liberate an Arab city that had originally liberated itself from a repressive central government in the midst of a brutal civil war reduced the extent to which U.S. forces could fully see and analyze dynamics on the ground and therefore ensure that all of the appropriate measures were taken to address civilian-harm concerns.[11] The Syrian government and its partners, Russia and Iran, provided no relief on this front and in fact took actions that made U.S. operations more difficult. Syrian government forces and their proxies at times targeted the U.S.-led coalition's primary partner on the ground, the SDF, across eastern Syria.[12] Russian and Syrian flight operations also complicated coalition operations and intelligence collection efforts. Despite agreed-upon deconfliction measures, violations occurred—for example, when Syrian aircraft engaged SDF ground positions.[13] Moreover, the risk to remotely piloted aircraft and long-range manned surveillance aircraft required constant evaluation. These risks at times led to flight denials and contributed to missed intelligence collection opportunities that would have otherwise supported battlefield-shaping operations and time-sensitive defensive operations and targeting that could have reduced risk to civilians.[14] This report focuses on U.S. actions in Raqqa, but the actions of the Syrian government and its Russian and Iranian partners undoubtedly contributed far more to civilian harm and suffering in Syria overall.

Fourth, Turkey's geopolitical interests in the region also created challenges that significantly constrained the coalition's military options. The SDF was led by the People's Protection Units (Yekîneyên Parastina Gel [YPG]), home-grown defense forces of Syria's Kurdish areas that emerged during Syria's civil war. The Turkish government views the YPG as deeply entwined with the Kurdistan Worker's Party (Partîya Karkerên Kurdistanê), which is a U.S.-designated foreign terrorist organization involved in an active insurgency and terrorism campaign against Turkish authorities.[15] In the lead-up to the battle for Raqqa, Turkey launched a

---

9 Although there is not a U.S. military doctrinal definition for *human terrain*, this idea most often refers to "the human population and society in the operational environment (area of operations) as defined and characterized by sociocultural, anthropologic, and ethnographic data and other non-geophysical information about that human population and society" (Jacob Kipp, Lester Grau, Karl Prinslow, and Don Smith, "The Human Terrain System: A CORDS for the 21st Century," *Military Review*, September–October 2006, p. 15; see also Joint Doctrine Note 4/13, *Culture and the Human Terrain*, London: U.K. Ministry of Defence, September 2013, p. 1-2). Information on human terrain is often unclassified and derived from open sources.

10 David R. Kogan, *The Coalition Military Campaign to Defeat the Islamic State in Iraq and Syria 21 AUG 2016–05 SEP 2017: The Sky Dragon Dismantles the "Caliphate,"* Combined Joint Task Force – Operation Inherent Resolve, 2017, p. 9.

11 "By, with, and through" is common shorthand for how U.S. forces leverage the security forces of allies and partners. That is, the United States indirectly supports some partners as they conduct their own operations, directly advises and fights alongside other partners, and supports and directs some partners to conduct operations as U.S. proxies.

12 Kogan, 2017, pp. 43–44.

13 Raqqah Study Group, *What the Battle for Raqqah Teaches the Force*, Fort George Meade, Md.: U.S. Army Asymmetric Warfare Group, March 13, 2018, pp. 25–27, Not available to the general public; and Kogan, 2017, pp. 44–55.

14 Raqqah Study Group, 2018, p. 27.

15 Bureau of Counterterrorism, *Country Reports on Terrorism 2019*, Washington, D.C.: U.S. Department of State, June 2020, pp. 60, 103, 242.

military operation against YPG units along the Syria-Turkey border to prevent the YPG from consolidating Kurdish territories. YPG commanders considered halting operations to seize the Tabqa Dam on their way to Raqqa in order to protect the Kurdish territories, but coalition leaders convinced them to press ahead toward Raqqa.[16] Turkey's threats and actions against the Kurds created a precarious operational environment and a Kurdish force that was willing to lead the fight to liberate Raqqa but was deeply uneasy about the vulnerabilities of its own territories within Syria. Turkey's potential for undermining U.S. objectives in the region and its role as a North Atlantic Treaty Organization ally led U.S. policymakers to delay and then limit the amount and types of support they would provide to the SDF, thereby impeding U.S. efforts to build the SDF into a more effective force. Nevertheless, the United States consistently emphasized that "the SDF was the only partner force that had the will and capacity necessary to defeat ISIS in Syria."[17]

Framing Civilian-Harm Issues

Although some of the strikes against ISIS targets early in OIR were preplanned, or deliberate, strikes usually against fixed targets as ground operations to liberate cities in Iraq and Syria began, the campaign was increasingly characterized by unplanned and unanticipated, or *dynamic*, strikes and strikes supporting partner forces under attack from ISIS (*troops-in-contact* strikes). Operations in Raqqa were characterized by an extremely high proportion of dynamic and troops-in-contact strikes in support of the SDF, as well as significant levels of civilian casualties and infrastructure damage.

Raqqa, in particular, serves as a cautionary tale about fighting at the nexus of counterterrorism, counterinsurgency, and conventional operations. The battle had all the ingredients for creating severe civilian-harm challenges:

- a city of poorly constructed, multi-story, concrete structures connected by secret tunnels between buildings and underground and narrow alleys that were easily obscured
- an enemy that was dug-in, capable, brutal, and desperate
- a coalition coordinating multiple countries and different U.S. military cultures—from the Air Force, special operations forces (SOF), and the U.S. Marine Corps (USMC)
- an insufficiently equipped partner ground force with few ties to the city it was trying to liberate.

The U.S. military's commitment to the law of war and to mitigating the risk of civilian harm drives its rules of engagement (ROE), which are extensive, sophisticated, and clear. Nevertheless, war creates competing risks that policymakers, military and civilian planners, and military operators must balance. Many humanitarian groups and other nongovernmental organizations (NGOs) work to document harm and advocate for civilian protection in the midst of conflict zones. Most of the NGO officials we interviewed respected DoD's commitment to mitigating civilian harm and its sophisticated approaches to operations but were nevertheless shocked at the scale of destruction in Raqqa. NGO officials argued that negotiat-

---

[16] Raqqah Study Group, 2018, p. 6; Kogan, 2017, pp. 39–40.

[17] Raqqah Study Group, 2018, p. 5; Kogan, 2017, p. 38.

ing evacuation corridors or pauses in fighting and operating with greater caution would have prevented civilian deaths and reduced long-term suffering caused by extensive infrastructure damage. The officials were also disappointed and puzzled by what they perceived as a lack of engagement on assessing and learning from civilian harm in the aftermath of the Raqqa operation. Most DoD officials, on the other hand, argued that mounting an aggressive operation to liberate Raqqa and destroy ISIS would reduce human suffering and do so more quickly, compared with a more cautious operation that allowed ISIS to remain embedded in Raqqa for a longer period and allowed more fighters to escape.[18]

Some of the tensions between DoD and NGO officials can be understood by framing civilian harm in the context of each group's expectations. Many DoD officials focus on technological and procedural improvements that help protect civilians while continuing to emphasize that civilian harm is an inevitable part of war. NGO officials, on the other hand, recognize these improvements but set the bar ever higher and aim to shine a bright light on every incident and report of civilian harm in order to clarify the human costs of conflict.

Successful operations in the 21st century have increased expectations about the U.S. military's ability to minimize civilian harm through technology and strategic superiority. As Sarah Sewall notes in her book *Chasing Success: Air Force Efforts to Reduce Civilian Harm*, "As advanced militaries showed that they could successfully employ force while causing fewer civilian deaths, observers came to expect such results."[19] U.S. capabilities to see the battlefield, identify and strike enemy targets, and adapt to enemy tactics have improved tremendously. At the same time, NGO personnel—as well as U.S. allies, members of Congress, and even many warfighters across U.S. military services—have adjusted upward their expectations of the U.S. military's role in responding to civilian-harm issues. At times, these expectations have been frustrated as the U.S. military has failed to sustain progress, primarily because of a poor institutional memory and a weak ability to learn from lessons, a phenomenon we observed in Raqqa operations.[20]

The decision to describe U.S. policy and military operations against ISIS in counterterrorism terms understated the challenges posed by an urban environment and ISIS tactics of hybrid warfare in Raqqa. These factors greatly affected how the military operation unfolded. For example, counterterrorism operations are often hyper-focused on one individual or small groups of fighters and informed by extended, intense intelligence collection and analytical resources dedicated to target selection and identification. The preparation phase prior to a counterterrorism operation draws on multiple levels of review and approval before launching a weapon. And even with a rigorous system of checks and balances, it is impossible to mitigate every contingency, given the imperfect nature of information and the extent to which humans are featured across every level of the military processes. The large-scale urban combat situations in Mosul and Raqqa provide important lessons about the role of operations and intelligence in relation to civilian harm during fast-paced, high-intensity conflicts.

---

[18] NGO officials, interview with the authors, February–August 2020; DoD officials, interview with the authors, March 2020, April 2020, November 2020.

[19] Sewall, 2016., p. 8.

[20] Sarah Sewall and Larry Lewis, *Reducing and Mitigating Civilian Casualties: Afghanistan and Beyond – Joint Civilian Casualty Study*, Washington, D.C.: Joint Center for Operational Analysis and U.S. Joint Forces Command, 2010, Not available to the general public; and Larry Lewis, Elizabeth Young, and Michael Messer, *Adaptive Learning for Afghanistan: Final Report*, Washington, D.C.: Joint and Coalition Operational Analysis, March 2011.

Importantly, the challenges of civilian harm in Raqqa that we identify in this report hint at the complexities of future conflict scenarios in which the United States might be involved. Specifically, the Raqqa experience provides valuable insights into the challenges posed by urban warfare and the associated risks of civilian harm, which are likely to characterize future combat scenarios with near-peer adversaries or competition with these adversaries through proxy military forces. Operational planning in the counterinsurgency campaigns launched in response to the threat of terrorism after the September 11, 2001, attacks benefited from levels of time and space that seem like a luxury when compared with the pace of Raqqa (or even higher-intensity conflicts) and persistent military operations that future near-peer combat are likely to require. It is therefore important to ask whether the United States and its allies are prepared to undertake the civilian-protection responsibilities and meet the expectations that will accompany these conflicts.

Study Purpose and Approach

We conducted this study in parallel with a congressionally directed RAND Corporation study on DoD's policies and procedures governing civilian casualty assessments, investigations, and responses. For the study described in this report, officials from the Office of the Secretary of Defense asked RAND to answer a concise yet complex two-part research question: What were the causes of civilian harm in Raqqa, and how can DoD reduce civilian harm in future operations?

To unpack this question, we organized our research into several lines of effort, which are reflected in the organization of this report. The first line of effort, documented in Chapter Two, analyzes DoD's policies and procedures for mitigating civilian harm. We analyzed DoD's application of the law of war and the guidance that DoD issues to meet—and often exceed—those requirements. We also studied DoD's targeting cycle, which helps improve DoD's ability to identify, track, and strike enemy combatants and then assess the results of those actions. The second line of effort, documented in Chapters Three and Four, contains a brief historical analysis of the battle for Raqqa, as well as a quantitative and qualitative analysis of the effects of the battle on civilians. We supplemented this research with analysis of unclassified satellite imagery, the bulk of which is documented in a separate annex, available online at www.rand.org/t/RRA753-1. The third line of effort, documented in Chapters Five through Ten, considers the challenges of civilian-harm mitigation in Raqqa from multiple perspectives: ISIS (Chapter Five); U.S. airpower (Chapter Six); U.S. ground units (Chapter Seven); U.S. efforts to work by, with, and through the SDF (Chapter Eight); U.S. intelligence efforts (Chapter Nine); and U.S. efforts to identify, assess, and respond to civilian-harm incidents (Chapter Ten). Chapter Eleven presents our findings and recommendations.

Study Methodology

Our data analysis was conducted along three lines of effort. We collected data relating to (1) DoD policies and procedures on the protection of civilians; (2) details about the battle for Raqqa; and (3) airpower, ground force, partnered operations, and intelligence challenges in Raqqa.

We analyzed several dozen DoD documents, most unclassified, with a focus on mitigating the risks of civilian harm. We also reviewed documents on assessing, investigating, and responding to civilian harm, including those related specifically to OIR and—for comparative purposes—those related to Operation Resolute Support in Afghanistan and operations in the U.S. Africa Command area of responsibility. Congressional legislation and report language were also valuable in providing insights about congressional interest and intent. U.S. Government Accountability Office reports, White House executive orders, and other U.S. government documents also provided useful context. And several reports and articles produced by NGOs and journalists provided important insights about civilian harm in OIR, international humanitarian law, the importance of transparency and accountability, and the perspectives of relief workers and the victims of civilian harm.

In addition, we conducted interviews with more than 80 officials from the Office of the Secretary of Defense, the Joint Staff, the Defense Security Cooperation Agency, the intelligence community, the U.S. Department of State, three military services, six combatant or component commands, and civil society organizations. Officials included active and retired senior military leaders, military planners and operators, DoD and State Department civilians, humanitarian policy experts and field workers, and journalists.

We also examined three types of unclassified quantitative data to understand the extent of civilian harm during the Raqqa operation. We used these quantitative data sources to analyze the military's kinetic activity, civilian casualties, and building damage in Raqqa. Next, we describe details about the quantitative data used for this report and their limitations.

CJTF-OIR Strike Data

We relied on data from CJTF-OIR, which issued "strike releases" for each day of the operation in Raqqa and throughout all of OIR. In Raqqa, the strike releases listed air and artillery strikes, engagements, and targets, denoted by location, for CJTF-OIR operations.[21] CJTF-OIR defined its terminology as follows:

- A *strike* was an administrative term that involved an approval from a target engagement authority for operators to conduct a single engagement or series of engagements against ISIS-affiliated forces in a designated geographic area.
- An *engagement* was an attack or series of attacks against ISIS-affiliated forces. An engagement may have had several targets.
- A *target* represented an ISIS-affiliated person, structure, or object intended for an engagement. A target may have had several joint desired points of impact, each of which may have involved one or more munitions.

These details were recorded by the U.S. military's controlling agency (strike cell, advisory cell, or Combined Air Operations Center) for each strike. However, not all of this information is publicly available, which created limitations in our unclassified analysis. As noted earlier, CJTF-OIR's daily strike releases included only the number of strikes, engagements, and targets; they did not include information on joint desired points of impact or munitions. Moreover, the term *strike* represents an aggregation and is not necessarily an accurate measure of the level of kinetic activity.

Thus, to accurately measure the level of kinetic activity in Raqqa over time, or to compare it with the level in other locations, we needed the data on the number of munitions employed.

[21] The way in which CJTF-OIR recorded strike data changed on April 21, 2017. Before that date, daily strike releases included only air strikes and deliberate artillery strikes; afterward, they included all artillery and air strikes. We acknowledge the change when considering comparisons between Raqqa and Mosul following April 21, 2017.

However, the munitions figures are not publicly available. Instead, we estimated the number of munitions used per day using the number of targets per day published by CJTF-OIR. We extrapolated munition estimates from target data by comparing total targets to munitions employed per month during the Mosul and Raqqa operations, data that CJTF-OIR provided to Airwars.[22] According to our analysis of those data, for each target reported in CJTF-OIR strike releases, the coalition used approximately three munitions on average. Although air or artillery strikes could drop dozens of munitions on a single target, this would likely be quite rare in the operation in Raqqa. Through our research, we found three munitions per target to be a fair estimate, and we use this baseline wherever munition estimates are listed in the report.

In addition, CJTF-OIR's publicly available data do not include the precise location of where a U.S. military action took place. For example, CJTF-OIR strike releases say that the coalition conducted strikes "near" Raqqa or "near" Abu Kamal. Targets that were recorded as "near" Raqqa and as taking place during the time frame of the Raqqa operation were considered, for the purposes of this study, to be targets that took place in Raqqa during the operation.

For all the reasons described here, we can draw only tentative conclusions in this report about what strike data say about any single operation on its own or relative to any other. Our analysis using these data can draw suggestive conclusions if all the available data point in a certain direction.

Civilian Casualty Data

We used available quantitative data to explore civilian casualties in Raqqa. Deaths or injuries from the coalition's military operations in Raqqa between June and October 2017 were counted as civilian casualties in this study.[23] Civilian casualty data are challenging to compile and vary by accuracy and likelihood of attribution to coalition actions. A single party's civilian casualty data set is insufficient to understand civilian harm in Raqqa. Therefore, we used several available sources to explore civilian casualties in Raqqa:

- *CJTF-OIR civilian casualty data.* CJTF-OIR released monthly reports of civilian casualties that it assessed to be, more likely than not, caused by U.S. military operations. As of November 2020, that number stood at 240 civilian casualties (178 killed, 62 wounded) in Raqqa from 38 different incidents.[24]
- *Airwars and Amnesty International data.* We also examined civilian casualty data reported by NGOs.[25] The most-complete and most-consistent NGO data on civilian casualties in Raqqa come from a joint effort between Airwars and Amnesty International. By using a combination of field interviews, satellite imagery, and coalition strike data, the NGOs categorized as "verified" 774 civilian casualties in Raqqa (744 killed, 30 wounded) likely

---

[22] Airwars received monthly munition data from CJTF-OIR and shared those data with RAND. See also Samuel Oakford, *Death in the City: High Levels of Civilian Harm in Modern Urban Warfare Resulting from Significant Explosive Weapons Use*, London: Airwars, May 2018; and NGO official, interview with the authors, August 2020.

[23] Explosive remnants of war were another significant source of civilian casualties in Raqqa in the aftermath of coalition military operations but were outside the scope of our study.

[24] RAND compiled and analyzed data from CJTF-OIR, "Strike Releases," webpage, undated.

[25] An in-depth study of civilian casualties by two journalists argues that the U.S. military's data undercount the number of civilian casualties caused by U.S. forces by a factor of four (Azmat Khan and Anand Gopal, "The Uncounted," *New York Times Magazine*, November 16, 2017).

caused by the coalition from 108 incidents.[26] The highest Airwars and Amnesty International estimate for the number of civilian casualties caused by coalition forces in Raqqa is more than 1,600.[27]

- *SDF data.* The previous two sources of civilian casualty data tabulate civilian casualties in Raqqa by coalition forces only. To fully understand the extent of civilian casualties during the operation, one needs a separate number—the total number of civilians killed in Raqqa. Through an NGO official based in northeastern Syria, we acquired data on the total number killed, as tallied by the SDF—the local partner of the coalition—as they were uncovered during the Raqqa operation. As of this writing, the SDF estimated that it uncovered 4,118 dead civilians in Raqqa during the operation, plus an additional 1,878 who appeared dressed in military gear.[28] Although this number likely helps us understand the scope of civilian harm, it provides only limited help in understanding the extent to which any other actor (e.g., ISIS) caused the deaths.

As with strike data, the challenges of cataloging the number of civilian casualties and their ultimate causes are complex and disputed. Thus, we compiled multiple sources that can result in only tentative conclusions and only when they all point to a similar result.

Importantly, in some places in this report, we focus on analyzing the number of civilian casualty *incidents* (i.e., incidents in which one or more civilians were killed or wounded) over the number of civilian casualties. We recognize that each life harmed is important and that there are important reasons to analyze civilian casualty data by the number of civilians harmed (i.e., studying why incidents with high civilian casualties occur). We chose to also consider data on civilian casualty incidents because they help us understand the overall risk of civilian harm.[29] Because it might be more effective to find ways to limit the number of civilian casualty incidents rather than the number of civilians killed in an incident, our analysis includes both.

Damage Data

RAND reviewed select battle damage assessments compiled by the U.S. military during the Raqqa operation. RAND found that the assessments (1) did not consistently contain sufficient information on collateral damage or civilian harm for our analysis and (2) did not provide a comprehensive roll-up of cumulative damage for particular areas of neighborhoods. Given these two factors, the battle damage assessments did not substantively contribute to our understanding of civilian harm in Raqqa and were not used.

Instead, we relied on satellite imagery analysis to understand the scope of building and infrastructure damage in Raqqa during the operation. To compile a baseline assessment of the total number of buildings damaged or destroyed, the United Nations compared satel-

---

[26] Amnesty International, Airwars, and local partners conducted a detailed study of civilian casualties in Raqqa, including three months of field work. Their verified estimates are of civilian casualties that they believe have the highest likelihood of being caused by the coalition. These estimates were informed by locally reported incidents and corroborated by satellite imagery and field visits. See Amnesty International, "War in Raqqa: Rhetoric Versus Reality," webpage, undated. Amnesty International staff shared their clean data from the joint study with us for this study.

[27] Amnesty International, undated.

[28] These numbers are from the SDF Initial Response Team's assessment of deceased civilians removed from Raqqa after the 2017 operation, which a Kurdish NGO worker shared with the authors in August 2020.

[29] For more detail on how to analyze civilian casualty incidents, see, for example, Larry Lewis, *Improving Lethal Action: Learning and Adapting in U.S. Counterterrorism Operations*, Arlington, Va.: CNA, September 2014.

lite images of Raqqa in February and October 2017.[30] Because the Raqqa operation occurred completely during this period, we rely on these statistics for a baseline assessment of the total amount of damage in the city. Where possible, we sought to compare the United Nations damage assessments with other available research. For example, we interviewed a researcher who worked on a damage and needs assessment after the Raqqa operation for the European Union. Although that report is not public, this researcher provided important feedback on the United Nations report. We also analyzed dozens of unclassified satellite images in and around Raqqa before, during, and after the battle to draw our own conclusions. These can be found in the online annex to this report.

Satellite image analysis is helpful for total damage assessments, but it does not easily differentiate among perpetrators of the damage. Even though the United States provided nearly all of the supporting fires during the operation, battle damage assessments cannot distinguish whether damage was caused by artillery rounds, air strikes, large-caliber weapons, or ISIS's homemade explosives. This means that, although we can assess the extent of damage in Raqqa during the operation, we cannot make claims about which party was responsible for the damage assessed, except sometimes on a case-by-case basis.

Study Limitations

There are several limitations to this study. First, although we provide some discussion of U.S. coalition partners and often refer to the 80-plus members of the international coalition in broad terms, the bulk of our research focused on U.S. policymakers and military forces and their SDF partners. Second, although we interviewed many people with on-the-ground experience in Raqqa, we did not interview civilian victims or their families, SDF or ISIS fighters, or local Raqqa officials. Third, although we reviewed DoD strike logs, battle damage assessments, and civilian casualty figures to perform a limited quantitative analysis of the effect of air and artillery munitions on civilian harm, comprehensive data were difficult to access and analyze for several reasons. For instance, the data are published individually; little to no tabular data on civilian harm exist that are declassified and released by the U.S. government. And the data that do exist are difficult to use. For example, as we noted in the section on methodology, the numbers of strikes and engagements listed in the CJTF-OIR strike releases do not provide sufficiently useful detail for analyzing the effect of munition use on civilian harm. We were able to use the number of targets listed in the CJTF-OIR strike releases but only after comparing those data against nonpublic data on munitions. Nonpublic data allowed for some analysis but also had important limitations. We tried to collect as much usable data as possible in this study, but DoD should do more to make its data useful to researchers from an institutional learning perspective. At present, civilian-harm data collected by the U.S. military is geared toward capturing individual incidents and assessments rather than helping draw broader analytical conclusions about trends or operations as a whole that could support longer-term learning objectives.

Finally, we did not try to adjudicate the discrepancies between DoD and NGO reporting, although we provide an analysis of why it was difficult to accurately assess civilian harm in Raqqa. Moreover, the challenges, findings, and recommendations we identify may not be generalizable to all conflict scenarios and do not represent all possible insights into this complex and ever-evolving topic.

---

[30] United Nations Institute for Training and Research, "Damage Density of Ar Raqqa, Ar Raqqa Governorate, Syria," map, Geneva, November 21, 2017.

CHAPTER TWO

DoD Policies and Procedures for Mitigating Civilian Harm

DoD strictly adheres to the law of war and has deep commitment to civilian protection. As we discuss in this chapter, the internationally accepted foundational principles of the law of war, along with additional DoD policies and procedures, emphasize the protection of civilians in combat and delineate mechanisms to mitigate civilian harm. In the operational environment, U.S. forces know that they must be able to characterize the enemy, friendly forces, and the civilian environment prior to making targeting decisions. Although U.S. forces are trained to consider every unknown object or person in the area of operations as "innocent until proven guilty," they are keenly aware of the threats that exist to individual soldiers and to the force as a whole.[1] Generally, this process works to protect friendly forces but can also pose a significant risk to civilians caught in the crossfire, particularly in conditions of urban combat. Despite DoD efforts to maintain and disseminate rigorous guidance on the importance of protecting civilians, as well as U.S. military commanders' deliberate efforts to communicate the mission-critical need to avoid civilian harm to their forces, U.S. military operations might unintentionally cause harm to civilians.

Law of War, Rules of Engagement, and Informal Mechanisms for Mitigating Civilian Harm

The law of war provides the foundational principles—military necessity, humanity, proportionality, distinction, and honor—for DoD's efforts to protect civilians during armed conflict.[2] The law of war is not a set of black-letter rules, and its application relies on military judgment and the context of combat operations. The *Department of Defense Law of War Manual* provides information on law of war concepts to U.S. commanders, legal practitioners, and other DoD personnel responsible for conducting military operations while working to protect civilians.[3] The manual also provides tools to legal practitioners in the field to support coherent, principled, and correct advice to operational commanders. The military services also have their own manuals on the law of war.[4]

---

[1] General officer and SOF operator, interview with the authors, July 2020.

[2] Office of the General Counsel, U.S. Department of Defense, *Department of Defense Law of War Manual*, Washington, D.C.: U.S. Department of Defense, December 2016, pp. 65–69.

[3] Office of the General Counsel, U.S. Department of Defense, 2016.

[4] For example, Field Manual 6-27, *The Commander's Handbook on the Law of Land Warfare*, Washington, D.C.: Department of the Army and Department of the Navy, August 2019; and Air Force Instruction 51-401, *The Law of War*, Department of the Air Force, August 3, 2018.

Above and beyond its law of war obligations, DoD implements policies and procedures at multiple levels to help protect civilians during armed conflict. U.S. government policy at the highest level directs departments and agencies to take measures to protect civilians in military operations. Executive Order 13732, issued on July 1, 2016, states that relevant agencies shall, consistent with mission objectives and applicable law, train personnel on the protection of civilians, field weapons, and ISR systems that contribute to civilian protection; take feasible precautions to reduce the likelihood of civilian casualties; review incidents involving civilian casualties; acknowledge responsibility for civilian casualties and offer condolences; and engage with foreign partners to share best practices, among other measures.[5]

The combatant commands also adhere to Secretary of Defense–approved and theater-specific ROE, which set forth the circumstances in which force may be used, as well as the limitations on its use. Authorities in the ROE establish which groups and individuals may be targeted because they have been declared hostile and which groups may be defended. The ROE, which are classified, reflect a variety of operational, policy, and legal considerations and are often more restrictive than the law of war. In addition to ROE, guidance around the issue of civilian harm is also communicated through what is known as *commander's intent*, which provides additional tailored direction regarding the use of force. Commander's intent may come in the form of tactical directives, special instructions, operational orders, fragmentary orders, or other informal means of communications. For example, U.S. Central Command (CENTCOM)'s Command Policy Letter No. 85, issued on September 1, 2016, provides the command's policy on civilian casualty mitigation. The policy directs all personnel involved in CENTCOM operations to continuously evaluate methodologies (including intelligence methodologies) to minimize civilian casualties, ensure that personnel are trained on the law of war, take all feasible precautions when conducting attacks to reduce the likelihood of civilian casualties, maintain open communication channels with NGOs that operate in conflict zones, and assess reports of potential civilian casualties.[6] On December 22, 2016, LTG Stephen J. Townsend, the CJTF-OIR commander, also issued Tactical Directive #1: Enabling Coalition Support to Partner Forces, which, among other things, emphasized the critical importance of minimizing civilian causalities and reinforced the ROE.[7]

The effect of Tactical Directive #1 on civilian-harm mitigation, however, is contested. The directive delegated target engagement authority (TEA)—the authority and responsibility to engage targets with fires—to lower echelons.[8] Townsend delegated TEA in a desire to avoid delays from coordinating approvals up and down chains of command, which can have a negative impact on military effectiveness. There was concern that this delegation of authority contributed to the rise in civilian casualties in Mosul and Raqqa.[9] In the Joint Staff's 2018 *Civilian Casualty (CIVCAS) Review*, conducted at the direction of Secretary of Defense Mattis and Chairman of the Joint Chiefs of Staff Joseph Dunford, the authors found that "the

---

[5] Executive Order 13732, "United States Policy on Pre- and Post-Strike Measures to Address Civilian Casualties in U.S. Operations Involving the Use of Force," White House, July 1, 2016.

[6] CENTCOM, *Civilian Casualty Policy*, Command Policy Letter No. 85, Tampa, Fla., September 1, 2016.

[7] Kogan, 2017, p. 24.

[8] Joint Publication 3-09, *Joint Fire Support*, Washington, D.C.: Joint Chiefs of Staff, April 10, 2019.

[9] Tom Vanden Brook, "New Rules Allow More Civilian Casualties in Air War Against ISIL," *USA Today*, April 19, 2016. The role of the TEA is described in further detail in Raqqah Study Group, 2018, p. 55.

delegation of Target Engagement Authority did not directly cause an increase in the rate of CIVCAS [civilian casualties] during OIR."[10] We believe that a more comprehensive analysis of this particular case—including the indirect implications of TEA delegation—might require more-detailed analysis of classified strike data to compare specific incidents resulting from decisions made at different echelons of TEA and the factors that contributed to civilian casualties. Two broader questions to consider, however, are whether the delegation of TEA to lower echelons inherently increases the risk of civilian casualties and how leaders, regardless of level, can ensure that the most-effective targeting takes place. It could be argued that any delegation of the TEA function increases the risk of civilian casualties. For example, higher echelons will have more-senior and potentially more-experienced commanders, and they can also have additional resources—such as intelligence sources or tools—to draw upon to make decisions.

However, these potential advantages are not definitive. There may be cases in which decentralizing authority can be a better choice. One historical example was in Iraq in 2008, when Multi-National Forces – Iraq faced attacks in the Green Zone from a politically sensitive location, Sadr City. Iraqi President Nouri al-Maliki had forbidden coalition operations in that area, but the Multi-National Forces – Iraq commander convinced him that operations, necessary for self-defense, could be performed with minimal harm to the population. One feature of these operations was a decentralization of TEA to the brigade level, because these forces had a better understanding of the operating environment and the human terrain. To support the delegation, resources that were normally controlled at the division level or higher were allocated to the brigade headquarters. The success of these operations demonstrated that delegation of TEA to lower echelons does not inherently increase risk. The associated risks of delegation can be successfully managed when resources and well-prepared leaders and operators are in place. Ultimately, determining the level for TEA will be context-specific.

The communication of commander's intent must balance many aspects of an operation, but it plays a critical role in translating broad guidance into ways for tactical units to avoid civilian-harm incidents during combat. For example, our interviews with commanders of USMC tactical units suggested that commander's intent around civilian harm is most effective when it is explicitly integrated into specific missions and tied directly to the accomplishment of strategic objectives for a particular operation or campaign.[11] As one commander explained, "as long as we tie [the civilian casualty issue] to the mission, it makes sense."[12] Moreover, commander's intent should be communicated regularly in the course of face-to-face interaction between leaders and junior troops so that it is passed down to the smallest unit levels.[13] Commander's intent is also a critical tool to increase unit awareness around the importance of reporting civilian casualty incidents and the processes and procedures in place to respond to such incidents.

DoD responsibilities around training and equipping U.S. forces also play a role in mitigating civilian harm during U.S. military operations. Training for U.S. forces addresses these topics at the strategic, operational, and tactical levels, including through courses on collateral damage estimation (CDE) for both U.S. and North Atlantic Treaty Organization military

---

[10] Joint Staff, *Civilian Casualty (CIVCAS) Review*, Washington, D.C., April 17, 2018.

[11] USMC tactical ground unit commander, interview with the authors, April 2020.

[12] U.S. military tactical unit operator, interview with the authors, April 2020.

[13] USMC tactical ground units, interview with the authors, March 2020, April 2020.

forces. Many militaries, including highly capable U.S. allies, use these products as models for their own guidance documents.[14] Decades of experience in diverse and intense battlefields have contributed to formalized processes and increasingly robust guidance around civilian harm, and many U.S. military components have developed their own approaches to training around the issue of civilian casualties.[15] USMC, for instance, integrates preventing and responding to civilian casualties into basic training required for officers, pre-deployment training programs, and ongoing training as units deploy overseas. At the Basic School, new officers receive training through scenario-based instruction methods that are considered the most effective in conveying the nuances of mitigating civilian harm during combat operations.[16] That said, many operators also stressed that there is still room to enhance training in these areas, particularly in how the joint force operates in complex, high-risk environments.

In sum, DoD's guidance on the use of force and strong emphasis on minimizing civilian harm is generally quite clear and strong. The next section discusses the processes and procedures around the targeting cycle, another important component of DoD's efforts to mitigate civilian harm.

Overview of the Targeting Cycle

The military's procedures for targeting comprise an important component of DoD efforts to mitigate civilian casualties. During the targeting process, the U.S. military analyzes and prioritizes potential targets to engage with fires, using a six-phase cycle by which operating forces develop, validate, and nominate targets as part of military operations (Figure 2.1).[17]

The targeting cycle applies to two types of strikes, referred to as deliberate and dynamic strikes. *Deliberate* strikes are conducted against targets that are known to exist in the operational environment and against which a strike is planned 24–72 hours in advance.[18] These typically occur to help shape future operations or ground force maneuver. By contrast, *dynamic* targeting is a more reactive process and occurs in a compressed time frame. Dynamic strikes can occur against three types of targets: those that are known but previously unplanned, those that are previously unanticipated, or those that are hit in scenarios of self-defense.[19] The distinction between deliberate and dynamic strikes is important because past studies estimate that the vast majority of civilian casualties occur from dynamic targeting.[20] As we discuss later in the report, most strikes in Raqqa were dynamic.

---

[14] DoD official, interview with the authors, April 2020; NGO official, interview with the authors, April 2020.

[15] USMC tactical unit operator, interview with the authors, March 2020.

[16] USMC tactical unit operators, interview with the authors, March 2020, April 2020; and The Basic School, *Law of War/ Introduction to Rules of Engagement B130936 Student Handout*, Camp Barrett, Va.: Marine Corps Training Command, undated.

[17] Joint Publication 3-60, *Joint Targeting*, Washington, D.C.: Joint Chiefs of Staff, September 28, 2018, Not available to the general public.

[18] Air Force Annex 3-60, *Targeting*, Washington, D.C.: Curtis E. LeMay Center for Doctrine Development and Education, March 15, 2019.

[19] Air Force Annex 3-60, 2019.

[20] Joint Staff, 2018, p. 5.

Figure 2.1
Joint Targeting Cycle

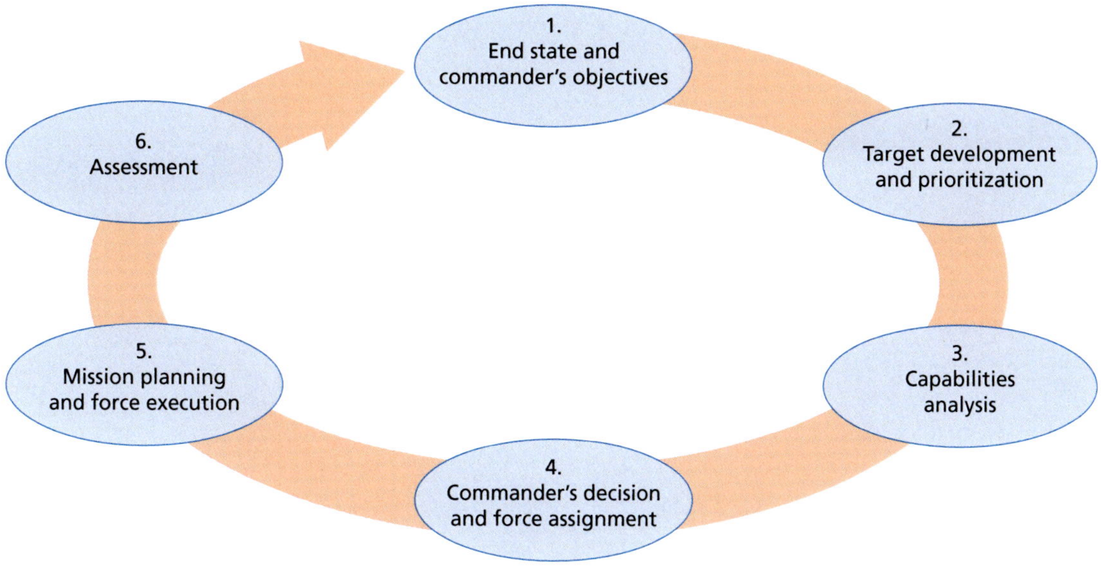

SOURCE: Joint Publication 3-60, *Joint Targeting*, Washington, D.C.: Joint Chiefs of Staff, January 31, 2013, p. II-4.

Concern for mitigating civilian harm is an integral feature of the targeting cycle. All targeting decisions, for example, must be made in light of the applicable ROE. Positive identification—reasonable certainty that the proposed target is a legitimate military target—is crucial to having a valid target. Objects identified as valid targets for engagement are subject to a CDE to predict the expected harm to civilians and civilian structures that specific munitions or methods of attack are likely to cause. However, a CDE is not required for all types of targets. For example, at the time of the Raqqa operation, formal CDE was required for all preplanned and some dynamic targets. In scenarios of coalition self-defense or partner force defense, formal CDE was not required; however, according to operators in OIR, it was often done informally.[21] Rules also govern which structures sites operators must place on a no-strike list; these are usually objects protected under international law, such as hospitals, civilian schools, or cultural sites.[22]

Our research shows that, although most U.S. military operators believe that they receive adequate guidance around the process for identifying individuals, groups, and structures as enemy targets, the mere existence of guidance is insufficient to effectively mitigate against the

---

[21] U.S. ground operator, interview with the authors, November 2020.

[22] These processes are documented in detail in Chairman of the Joint Chiefs of Staff Instruction 3160.01C (Chairman of the Joint Chiefs of Staff Instruction 3160.01C, *No-Strike and Collateral Damage Estimation Methodology*, Washington, D.C.: Joint Chiefs of Staff, 2018, Not available to the general public). Chairman of the Joint Chiefs of Staff Instruction 3370.01B further delineates the relationship between CDE and the target identification and development process to determine valid military targets from no-strike objects and how to mitigate civilian harm (Chairman of the Joint Chiefs of Staff Instruction 3370.01B, *Target Development Standards*, Washington, D.C.: Joint Chiefs of Staff, May 6, 2016, Not available to the general public).

potential for civilian harm.[23] Because targeting falls at the intersection of intelligence, operations, and planning (see Figure 2.2.), and because TEAs may be situated at lower levels of command depending on conflict dynamics, there are several opportunities to better adapt the targeting process and targeting tools to account for civilian harm.

Tools for Reducing Civilian Harm

Given the complexity of targeting, it may be helpful to break down some of its components into categories that can be analyzed through the lens of civilian-harm mitigation. Some of the same tools that are used to improve targeting for mission effectiveness are also crucial for reducing civilian harm. Understanding how these tools were applied in Raqqa and elsewhere may help identify ways that operators and analysts can better prepare for future missions.

Drawing from the discussion in the previous section, Table 2.1 reviews several aspects of targeting that can be viewed as tools for reducing civilian-harm mitigation and that were applied in Raqqa.

In sum, the integration of robust formal and informal structures and practices into the targeting cycle and the improved preparation for using targeting tools in joint and partnered operations are likely to improve U.S. military operators' pre-strike awareness, post-strike

Figure 2.2
Targeting Overview

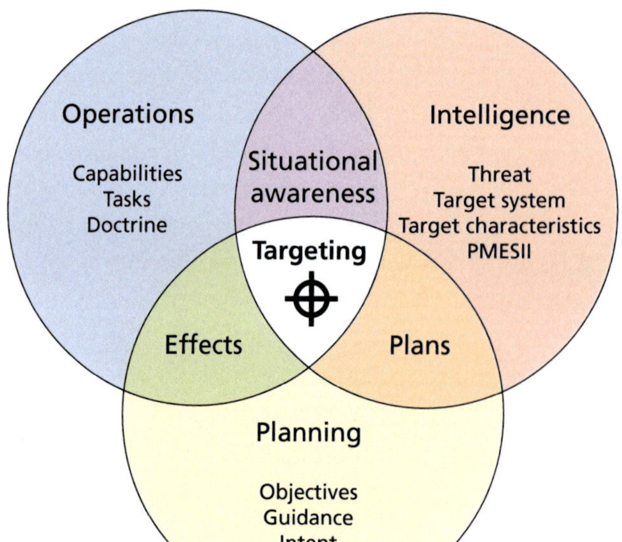

SOURCE: Joint Publication 3-60, 2013, p. I-6.
NOTE: PMESII = political, military, economic, social, information, and infrastructure.

[23] U.S. military tactical unit operators, interview with the authors, April 2020, May 2020, June 2020. In addition, the 2018 Joint Staff Civilian Casualty Review concluded that DoD's positive identification process for OIR had sufficient guidance and structure (see Joint Staff, 2018, p. 6).

Table 2.1
Targeting and Civilian-Harm Mitigation Tools

Category	Tools for Reducing Civilian Harm	Application to Raqqa
CDE	CDE predicts expected civilian harm.	• CDE was not required for self-defense situations but was often done informally anyway.
Target development	ISR can be used to confirm patterns of life around potential targets, identifying where noncombatants may be present.	• A minimum number of full-motion video hours were required prior to nominating deliberate targets. • ISR assets were prioritized for operations in Mosul, which limited target development immediately prior to the start of the Raqqa operation. • Because many strikes in Raqqa were dynamic and often executed under self-defense ROE, full target development often did not occur.
Civilian-harm assessment	By viewing civilian-harm incidents as an integral part of the targeting cycle rather than as discrete events, lessons can be shared among units and institutionalized for future learning.	• Some unit commanders said that they emphasized civilian-harm assessments as learning tools in Raqqa but noted that other commanders did not. • Lessons from concurrent operations in Mosul were sometimes shared with units engaged in Raqqa to help mitigate civilian-harm risks.
TEA	TEA can be limited by rank, nationality, or access to information, which can help manage risk.	• In Raqqa, the joint force commander delegated TEA to lower echelons, which created advantages (agility, ground-level awareness) and disadvantages (reduced strategic situational awareness, inexperience, fewer resources available).
Weaponeering	Low-yield weapons and delayed fuses are common tools for limiting collateral damage from air strikes. Using precision guidance kits is a tool to increase the precision of artillery strikes.	• Pilots employed Joint Direct Attack Munition kits to minimize civilian harm. The extensive use of these weapons in OIR at times led to shortages, resulting in the Air Force drawing on stocks from other theaters. Pilots also selected delayed fusing for weapons to minimize the amount of fragmentation of the bomb. • Many artillery fires were for terrain denial, obscuration (i.e., smoke), and illumination—circumstances in which precision guidance kits were generally not employed.
Use of joint tactical air controllers (JTACs)	JTACs are service members who direct the action of combat aircraft engaged in close air support and other offensive air operations from a forward position.	• In Iraq, U.S. forces worked with certified JTACs in Iraq's Counter Terrorism Service. In Syria, U.S. JTACs were not permitted to be on the front lines in Raqqa, and the SDF were not permitted to act as JTACs. Thus, U.S. forces had higher requirements for corroborating SDF targets. • To automate the transmission of data and help create a common operational picture, the coalition provided the SDF with Android Tactical Assault Kits.

assessments, and overall learning about the complexities inherent to mitigating civilian harm. Improving how and when leaders and operators across DoD share their experiences with civilian-harm issues from Afghanistan, Iraq, and elsewhere will set them up to benefit from the hard-learned lessons of the few, ultimately minimizing mistakes from the beginning of each person's targeting-related assignment. Incorporating these lessons into training is also critically important because combat operations and associated battlefield experiences have decreased.

CHAPTER THREE

The Battle for Raqqa: Overview and Operational Approach

This chapter provides a narrative of the 2017 Raqqa operation and is divided into two sections. The first section describes conditions in Raqqa at the outbreak of Syria's civil war. The second section outlines the battle to capture Raqqa, ending with the negotiated departure of ISIS fighters in October 2017.

The City Before the Battle for Raqqa

Background on Raqqa (March 2011–June 2017)

Raqqa is strategically situated on the Euphrates River in Syria's fertile north, part of the Middle East's larger contested Fertile Crescent. Raqqa is a key crossroads in Syria: It straddles both major highways that connect Turkey, northern Syria, and Iraq and that provide access to the Deir ez-Zor Governorate's oil fields.[1] Raqqa is considered an agricultural "secondary city"—the largest city in Syria's northern agricultural region and home to large cotton and grain industries.[2] Figure 3.1 shows a satellite image of Raqqa and its surroundings in January 2013. For more information on our geospatial intelligence analysis and the maps used in this report, see the online annex.

Two major bridges cross the Euphrates south of Raqqa city: the older al-Mansour (or Eastern) Bridge and the new Raqqa (Western) Bridge connecting newer, planned developments in western Raqqa. These bridges link Raqqa to agricultural fields and to highways leading to urban centers in the west (Aleppo) and east (Deir ez-Zor).[3]

Prior to the start of Syria's civil war in 2011, densely packed residential neighborhoods stood next to businesses, mosques, clinics, pharmacies, banks, and schools in much of Raqqa, and especially in the city center.[4] During the battle for Raqqa, ISIS fighters would ultimately use this dense, centralized urban infrastructure to their advantage, employing civilians as human shields and taking over hospitals, clinics, apartment complexes, and schools to defend themselves.

---

1 Rachel Kreisman, "Raqqa and the Oil Economy of ISIS," Atlantic Council, May 15, 2017.

2 Brian Roberts and Rene Peter Hohmann, "The Systems of Secondary Cities: The Neglected Drivers of Urbanising Economies," Cities Alliance, CIVIS No. 7, 2014.

3 Unpublished 2016 RAND research on roads and infrastructure for Raqqah stabilization, by Howard J. Shatz, Jeffrey Martini, Eric Robinson, James Dobbins, Daniel Egel, Sean Mann, and Charles P. Reis.

4 On Raqqa's complex, highly residential-oriented organization, see neighborhood profile descriptions in REACH Initiative, "Situation Overview: Area-Based Assessment of Ar-Raqqa City," Geneva, March 2018, pp. 20–26.

Figure 3.1
Raqqa and Its Environs, January 2013

SOURCES: Google Earth Pro, Maxar Technologies; OpenStreetMap.

Syrian Opposition Captures Raqqa (March 2013)

On March 6, 2013, an alliance of Syrian armed opposition groups captured Raqqa with relatively little fighting.[5] A brief period of revolutionary opposition governance emerged during spring 2013,[6] and it was during this period that the most-intense Syrian Arab Republican Government air strikes occurred, likely to undermine local faith in the opposition-led municipal government.[7] The Syrian Arab Republican Government deployed a combination of unguided and guided rockets and incendiary, barrel, and thermobaric bombs, the latter of which included both fuel-air explosives and vacuum bombs.[8] Damage caused by these relatively small-scale

---

[5] Eric Robinson, Daniel Egel, Patrick B. Johnston, Sean Mann, Alexander D. Rothenberg, and David Stebbins, *When the Islamic State Comes to Town: The Economic Impact of Islamic State Governance in Iraq and Syria*, Santa Monica, Calif.: RAND Corporation, RR-1970-RC, 2017, pp. 104–105.

[6] Nate Rosenblatt and David Kilcullen, *How Raqqa Became the Capital of ISIS: A Proxy Warfare Case Study*, Washington, D.C.: New America, July 25, 2019, p. 17.

[7] Rosenblatt and Kilcullen, 2019.

[8] Amnesty International has suggested but not confirmed that many of these attacks were undertaken by Syrian Air Force MiG-29s upgraded via a Russian Aircraft Corporation maintenance, repair, and operations base at Mezze Air Base near Damascus, first opened on the eve of the Syrian civil war in 2011. See Amnesty International, *Al-Raqqa Under Attack: Syrian Airforce Strikes Against Civilians*, London, 2015, p. 6.

but highly lethal devices can be difficult to identify via satellite imagery; some thermobaric devices, for instance, are specifically designed to kill people and destroy buildings through their vacuum-creating shockwaves and do not leave major craters when detonated in open spaces (see the geospatial intelligence review of this in the online annex, Section Two).[9] Overall, the level of damage in Raqqa caused by the Syrian Arab Republican Government after it lost control of the city was relatively minor compared with what occurred under ISIS control and the damage caused during coalition military operations to liberate the city from ISIS. However, this was likely the product of the Syrian Arab Republican Government's limited capacity to inflict damage on Raqqa and its relative lack of strategic interest in the city rather than any desire to intentionally limit civilian harm.

ISIS-Held Raqqa (January 2014–June 2017)

Raqqa was ISIS's beachhead in Syria—the first territory the group controlled in Syria's civil war. ISIS agents started infiltrating Raqqa in April 2013 and assumed complete control of the city by January 2014. Once it captured the city, ISIS helped rebuild some of the city's essential civilian infrastructure.[10] By July 2014, however, resident attitudes toward ISIS had soured.[11] Living standards had collapsed by the end of 2014, and ISIS rule over Raqqa from 2014 to 2017 was marred by horrific civilian-harm abuses, as evidenced by the mass graves of thousands of people uncovered after the city was captured by coalition forces in 2017.[12]

During its control of Raqqa, ISIS rarely destroyed civilian infrastructure; its abuses were less visible from satellite imagery. When it did destroy buildings, ISIS targeted symbolically important structures that it deemed blasphemous or suspected to be used for purposes that threatened its authority (e.g., Raqqa's Uwais al-Qarni mosque, a Shi'ite mosque, on March 26, 2014; see the online annex, Section Three).[13] Starting on September 22, 2014, the United States and key coalition partners, notably France and the United Kingdom, began striking known ISIS targets in Raqqa. Targets included intelligence-confirmed ISIS offices, leadership houses, and critical transportation and military infrastructure. However, with several exceptions, air strikes on Raqqa were infrequent for the rest of 2014 and up until the start of 2017.

ISIS fighters inflicted tremendous civilian harm in Raqqa before 2017, which is beyond the scope of this report. The extent to which ISIS inflicted civilian harm during the 2017 operation to capture Raqqa is covered in Chapter Five.

---

[9] Ben Watson, "Weapons of the Syrian War: Airpower (Syrian)," *Defense One*, July 19, 2016; Mary Wareham, "Dispatches: Incendiary Weapons Pose Civilian Threat in Syria," Human Rights Watch, June 21, 2016; Human Rights Watch, *Syria's Use of Incendiary Weapons: Memorandum to Convention on Conventional Weapons Delegates*, New York, November 2013, pp. 6–9; and Torie Rose DeGhett, "A New Kind of Bomb Is Being Used in Syria and It's a Humanitarian Nightmare," *Vice*, August 28, 2015.

[10] Robinson et al., 2017, pp. 105–108.

[11] Rosenblatt and Kilcullen, 2019.

[12] Heather Murdock, "Syrian Authorities Find 5,000 Bodies in Raqqa Mass Graves," Voice of America, September 4, 2019.

[13] Dimitar Mihaylov, "Cracks in the Crescent: The Looming Sectarian Clash Between Khilafah and Imamah," *Israel Journal of Foreign Affairs*, Vol. 9, No. 1, 2015, p. 58.

The Battle for Raqqa (June 6, 2017–October 20, 2017)

Battle for Raqqa: Isolation Phase

In November 2016, one month after coalition and Iraqi forces began to attack ISIS in Mosul, the SDF announced the beginning of the operation that it called the Wrath of the Euphrates. U.S. Army Special Operations Command, which originally designed the operation to capture Raqqa, called it Operation Eclipse. The operation was the largest irregular warfare campaign led by U.S. Army Special Operations Command since the 2001 invasion of Afghanistan. Capturing Raqqa was the coalition's primary objective in Syria in 2017, and the campaign led by Special Operations Joint Task Force (SOJTF)-OIR would eventually unfold in four phases, starting in November 2016 and concluding in October 2017 with the encirclement and multi-axis assault on Raqqa that resulted in capturing the city. U.S. SOF were involved in limited training of SDF ground forces, working out battle plans during the fight and facilitating fires support. However, SOF operators were rarely, if ever, in the city and did not fight on the front lines.[14]

SOJTF-OIR is a subcomponent of CJTF-OIR and was the lead planning element in the battle to capture Raqqa. Various USMC units, including artillery and infantry elements from the 11th and 24th Marine Expeditionary Units and the USMC Special Purpose Marine Air-Ground Task Force – Crisis Response – Central Command, also provided support.[15] In addition, 5,000 paratroopers from the Army's 82nd Airborne Division were stationed in Kuwait and ready to deploy to either Syria or Iraq if needed.[16] Although U.S. Department of State and U.S. Agency for International Development (USAID) teams were forward-deployed to northeast Syria in June 2017 as a humanitarian presence, they were not significantly involved in any operational planning with regard to mitigating civilian harm.[17]

A formal cap allowing a maximum of 503 U.S. troops in Syria remained in place at the start of the Raqqa operation.[18] That said, commanders reportedly retained the authority to temporarily exceed that limit and likely did so in March 2017, when an additional 400 troops were deployed to Syria to prepare "logistical and fire support to enable a successful assault on Raqqa."[19] One public estimate published at the start of the campaign suggests that there were between 500 and 900 U.S. forces forward-deployed to support the SDF in Raqqa in early 2017.[20] By the end of the operation, 2,000 U.S. forces were officially deployed to Syria.[21]

---

[14] Senior military officers and a retired senior military officer, interview with the authors, July 2020.

[15] Dan Lamothe and Thomas Gibbons-Neff, "Marines Have Arrived in Syria to Fire Artillery in the Fight for Raqqa," *Washington Post*, March 8, 2017; and U.S. military tactical unit operators, interview with the authors, April 2020, May 2020.

[16] Joseph V. Micallef, "Sitrep Raqqa: The Geopolitics of Eastern Syria," Military.com, June 26, 2017.

[17] Former U.S. official, interview with the authors, July 14, 2020; U.S. government humanitarian officials, correspondence with the authors, October 2020.

[18] Michael R. Gordon, "U.S. Is Sending 400 More Troops to Syria," *New York Times*, March 9, 2017a.

[19] Gordon, 2017a.

[20] Micallef, 2017.

[21] Dan Lamothe, "There Are Four Times as Many U.S. Troops in Syria as Previously Acknowledged by the Pentagon," *Washington Post,* December 6, 2017. Other sources put the number closer to 4,000 (Shawn Snow, "4,000 US Troops in Syria?" *Military Times*, October 31, 2017). At least 200 U.S. forces were stationed at the al-Tanf garrison along the Syria-Jordan-Iraq border and would not have operational relevance to the Raqqa operation (Sune Engel Rasmussen and Michael R. Gordon, "A Small U.S. Base Gets in Iran's Way—but Maybe Not for Long," *Wall Street Journal*, December 27, 2018).

SOJTF-OIR brought obvious strengths to the planning for Raqqa but also introduced important weaknesses. In terms of strengths, SOF units understood ISIS better than conventional forces did, because they had been fighting ISIS's predecessor organization, al-Qa'ida in Iraq, since the early 2000s. Moreover, U.S. SOF had been working with SDF elements since 2014 and intimately understood the by, with, and through approach to working with SDF fighters who would serve as the tip-of-the-spear ground force in Raqqa.[22] In terms of weaknesses, however, SOJTF-OIR had limited experience planning what was essentially a conventional combined arms urban combat operation supported by perhaps unprecedented (for them) levels of air and artillery strikes.[23] Moreover, as is detailed in Chapter Five, SOJTF-OIR did not bring a fully staffed operational-level headquarters with all the warfighting functions (e.g., an Army division headquarters) to lead the operational-level warfighting activities, such as targeting operations, needed for battlefield-shaping ahead of maneuver.

There were few humanitarian actors active in Raqqa as the operation unfolded. Limited by Syria's complex political environment, the United Nations was not leading the humanitarian response in Raqqa. Instead, a loose coalition of NGOs that organized into the North Eastern Syria NGO Forum were involved in much of the humanitarian assistance during the Raqqa operation; however, they operated with "minimal resources/footprint."[24]

Internationally, the Global Coalition to Defeat ISIS included more than 80 members, some of which were on the ground and carried out air strikes alongside the United States.[25] British and French SOF were reportedly present on the ground in Raqqa, and British and French air forces also launched air strikes during the combat operations to retake Raqqa in 2017.[26] However, the United States conducted an estimated 95 percent of the total air strikes during the Raqqa operation and all of the artillery strikes.[27] Although other countries had struck ISIS targets in Raqqa before the 2017 operation, they were not meaningfully involved in the battle for Raqqa.[28]

By the start of the operation to capture Raqqa city, in May 2017, an OIR spokesperson stated that the total force of the SDF numbered approximately 50,000 fighters, divided almost evenly between Syrian Kurds and Syrian Arabs.[29] According to one report at the time, 30,000 of the 50,000 fighters belonged to Kurdish units, including the YPG (and its affiliated all-

---

22 Senior military officers, interview with the authors, July 2020.

23 Former senior defense department official, interview with the authors, March 3, 2020; former senior military official, interview with the authors, May 7, 2020.

24 U.S. government humanitarian officials, correspondence with the authors, October 2020; United Nations official involved in coordinating aid for Raqqa, interview with the authors, August 2020.

25 The full list of anti-ISIS coalition partners is available from Global Coalition Against Daesh, "Partners," webpage, undated.

26 "IS Conflict: Coalition Strikes on Raqqa 'Killed 1,600 Civilians,'" BBC News, April 25, 2019.

27 NGO officials, interview with the authors, August 2020; CJTF-OIR, undated; and U.K. Ministry of Defence, "British Forces Air Strikes in Iraq and Syria: Monthly List," webpage, September 5, 2018a.

28 Helene Cooper and Eric Schmitt, "Airstrikes by U.S. and Allies Hit ISIS Targets in Syria," *New York Times*, September 22, 2014.

29 Congressional Research Service, *Armed Conflict in Syria: Overview and U.S. Response*, Washington, D.C., RL33487, August 2017. This figure represents the total force of the SDF; not all personnel participated in the operation to capture Raqqa from ISIS.

female militia), Asaish, and the region's self-defense forces.[30] The remaining 20,000 fighters belonged to various Arab militias, including Liwa Suqour al-Raqqa, a militia from Tabqah (a city near Raqqa), and Liwa Thuwar al-Raqqa, a militia from Raqqa.[31]

Inside Raqqa, approximately 30,000–40,000 SDF fighters, supported by coalition forces, led the fight and provided the bulk of the ground forces involved in the campaign. When it began its assault to capture the city on June 6, 2017, the SDF faced an ISIS force estimated at between 2,900 and 5,600 fighters (Table 3.1).[32]

In the initial two weeks of the operation, the SDF captured the sparsely populated neighborhoods on the outskirts of Raqqa city and forced ISIS to withdraw to the city's more densely populated central neighborhoods. By the end of the first month of the operation, the SDF had captured 35–40 percent of Raqqa and fully encircled the city with support from coalition forces (see Figure 3.2).[33]

Table 3.1
Combatants in the Battle for Raqqa

Combatant Force	Force Size at the Outset of the Battle	Number of Casualties at the Battle's End	Notes
U.S. and international coalition	500–900[a]	1[b]	There were an estimated 3,000–5,000 U.S. troops in Syria during the battle to capture Raqqa.[c]
SDF	30,000–40,000[d]	655[e]	As much as 70 percent of the SDF were ethnically Arab.[f] However, SDF command and tip-of-the-spear forces in Raqqa were predominantly Kurdish.[g]
ISIS	2,900–5,600[h]	1,400 (est.)[i]	250 ISIS fighters (and 3,500 ISIS family members) were evacuated to eastern Syria on October 15 as terms of their surrender of the city.[j]

[a] Micallef, 2017.

[b] CJTF-OIR combatant casualty counts, shared with the authors.

[c] Micallef, 2017.

[d] Micallef, 2017.

[e] People's Defense Units, "SDF Statement on the Raqqa Victory and the Future of the City," October 20, 2017.

[f] Micallef, 2017.

[g] State Department officials, interview with the authors, October 2020; DoD officials, interview with the authors, July, 2020, August 2020; Kurdish and Arab journalists and activists in Raqqa, interview with the authors, July 2020.

[h] Kogan, 2017, p. 38; and John Dorrian, "Department of Defense Press Briefing by Col. Dorrian via Teleconference from Baghdad, Iraq," transcript, U.S. Department of Defense, May 3, 2017c.

[i] Syrian Observatory for Human Rights, "Raqqa City: General Security After ISIS," October 20, 2018.

[j] Quentin Sommerville and Riam Dalati, "Raqqa's Dirty Secret," BBC News, November 13, 2017b.

---

30 Genevieve Casagrande, "The Road to Ar-Raqqah: Background on the Syrian Democratic Forces," Institute for the Study of War Backgrounder, November 22, 2016.

31 Raqqa journalist reporting on Arab militias fighting with the SDF, interview with the authors, June 2020.

32 Micallef, 2017.

33 "US-Backed Fighters Move into ISIS Stronghold Raqqa for the First Time," *The World*, June 6, 2017; Syrian Observatory for Human Rights, "'Euphrates Wrath' Operation Forces Control About 35% of Al-Raqqah City's Area and Prepare for the Conclusive Battle," July 12, 2017; and Chris Tomson, "ISIS Fully Encircled in Raqqa City After Latest Kurdish Advances," Al-Masdar News, June 24, 2017.

Figure 3.2
Raqqa Battle Progression

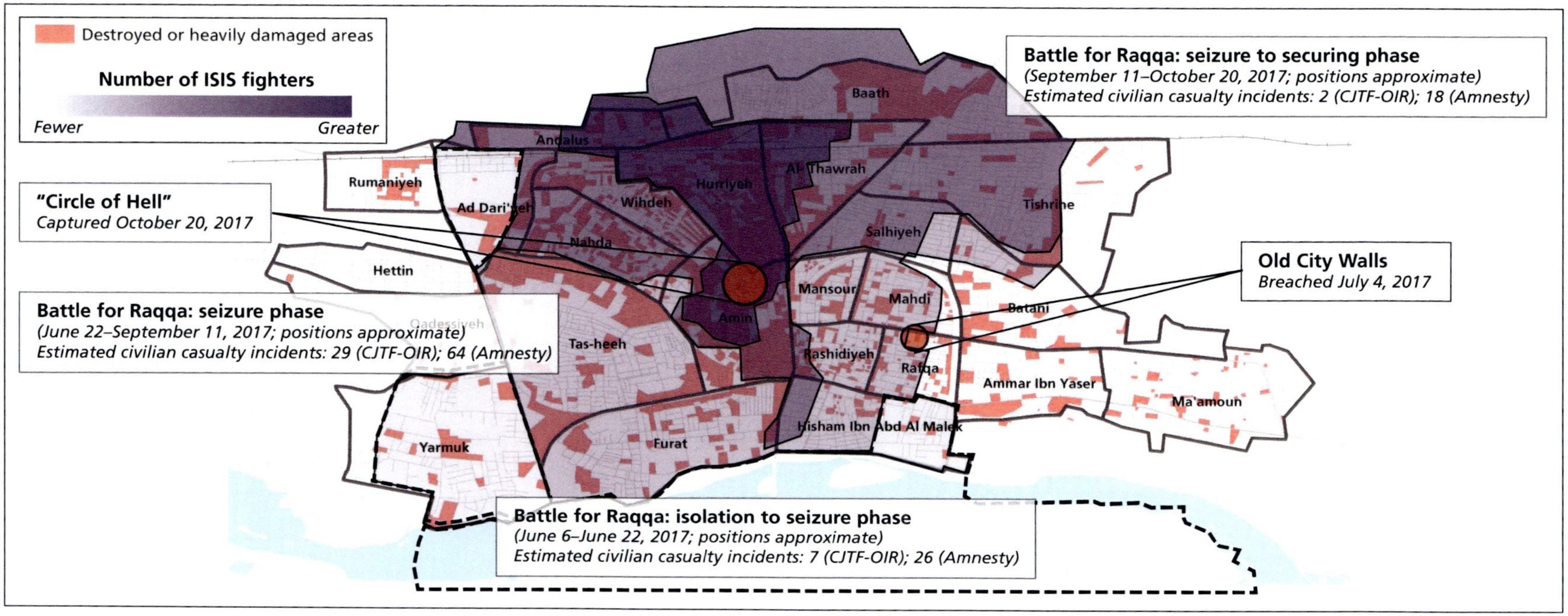

SOURCES: The base map is from REACH Initiative, "Ar-Raqqa City, Syria—Situation Overview VI," Geneva, October 13, 2017, map 5. Sources for our overlays on the map are Kogan, 2017; Walid Al Nofal, Mohammad Abdulssattar Ibrahim, and Mateo Nelson, "'1km' Remains for Syrian Democratic Forces to Completely Isolate Raqqa City," *Syria Direct*, June 22, 2017; Mohammad Abdulssattar Ibrahim and Mateo Nelson, "A 'Shift' in Strategy in Raqqa City amid Rising Civilian, Military Toll," *Syria Direct*, July 18, 2017a; Mohammad Abdulssattar Ibrahim and Mateo Nelson, "Islamic State Pushes Back Against SDF Advances in Southern Raqqa City," *Syria Direct*, August 1, 2017b; and "Syria War: UN Says It Is Ready to Go into Raqqa," BBC, October 18, 2017. Organizations in parentheses indicate the source of the civilian casualty data: *CJTF-OIR* indicates civilian casualty incidents that were considered "credible" by CJTF-OIR; *Amnesty* indicates civilian casualty incidents that were considered "verified" by Amnesty International's field work (Amnesty shared results with the authors).

NOTE: This figure shows the progression of phases in the battle for Raqqa and the location of ISIS forces in and around the area. The three phases were isolation, seizure, and securing. The purple shading indicates the concentration of ISIS forces at each phase (the darker the shading, the higher the concentration of ISIS forces). As the phases progressed, the amount of Raqqa that ISIS controlled decreased.

Battle for Raqqa: Transition from Isolation to Seizure Phase

By July 2017, ISIS fighters had retreated inside Raqqa's densely populated central neighborhoods, where the main phase of the battle would endure until late September. In the beginning of July, the SDF began operations to enter Raqqa city from the west, south, and east. In its progression from the west, the SDF faced many challenges because ISIS had heavily mined neighborhoods in that part of the city. In response, the SDF shifted to moving in from the east and crossed the Euphrates River from the south, eventually breaching the city limits in August 2017 (see Figure 3.2).[34]

From the east, the SDF faced stiff resistance from ISIS defenses constructed along Raqqa's historic, 2,500-meter Old City wall. On July 3, as SDF fighters tried to breach the wall, ISIS attacked them with vehicle-borne improvised explosive devices, mortars, heavy machine guns, grenades, and snipers. On July 4, in a coordinated action, the coalition conducted precision strikes to reduce two 25-meter sections of the Old City wall. These strikes enabled the SDF to breach the wall and enter the Old City. Although ISIS used the wall as a defensive position, the coalition took great care to minimize damage to the culturally significant structure.[35]

Once the SDF entered Raqqa's Old City, it engaged in intense, block-by-block fighting with ISIS from mid-July until the end of September 2017. Coalition strikes against presumed residential structures in the Old City deserve special consideration. Satellite imagery of one city block immediately south of the Harun al-Rashid fortress ruins in the Mahdi neighborhood showed that coalition forces targeted individual buildings as the situation on the ground evolved (Figure 3.3). Between the start of the battle and July 18, 2017, coalition forces targeted a single building on the block's northeast corner. The following week, the coalition targeted an adjacent interior building but otherwise left the rest of the block intact. A third building, this time on the block's western side, was eliminated between July 24 and August 12, 2017, forming a line of targeted buildings that cut across the block as coalition-backed SDF personnel fought building by building to control the Old City in early to mid-August 2017. This pattern suggests that ISIS militants were (1) moving positions across the block, (2) in control of individual buildings, or both, thereby requiring dynamic strikes in support of SDF ground maneuver. The block was captured by the SDF between mid-August and early September 2017.[36]

In addition to retreating into the Old City block by block, ISIS fighters made use of tunnels to advance across the front lines and attack from behind. For example, on August 14, ISIS launched a counterattack that involved the coordinated use of tunnels to attack the SDF at multiple locations: "ISIS has had time to rig up thousands of fiendishly clever explosives and to dig extensive tunnels. In the last two days, ISIS mounted a planned counterattack through these tunnels," explained OIR Spokesperson COL Ryan Dillon.[37] Following the failed counterattack, ISIS retreated further into the city, with its remaining territory consisting mainly of the Old City and other neighborhoods in north-central Raqqa.

---

34 Kurdish civilian activist who was a direct observer in the battle, interview with the authors, July 1, 2020.

35 CJTF-OIR, "SDF Breaches Old City of Raqqah," news release, July 4, 2017b.

36 Kogan, 2017, p. 42.

37 Ryan Dillon and Adam Stump, "Department of Defense Press Briefing by Colonel Dillon via Teleconference from Baghdad, Iraq," transcript, U.S. Department of Defense, August 16, 2017.

Figure 3.3
Block-by-Block Fighting in Raqqa's Old City

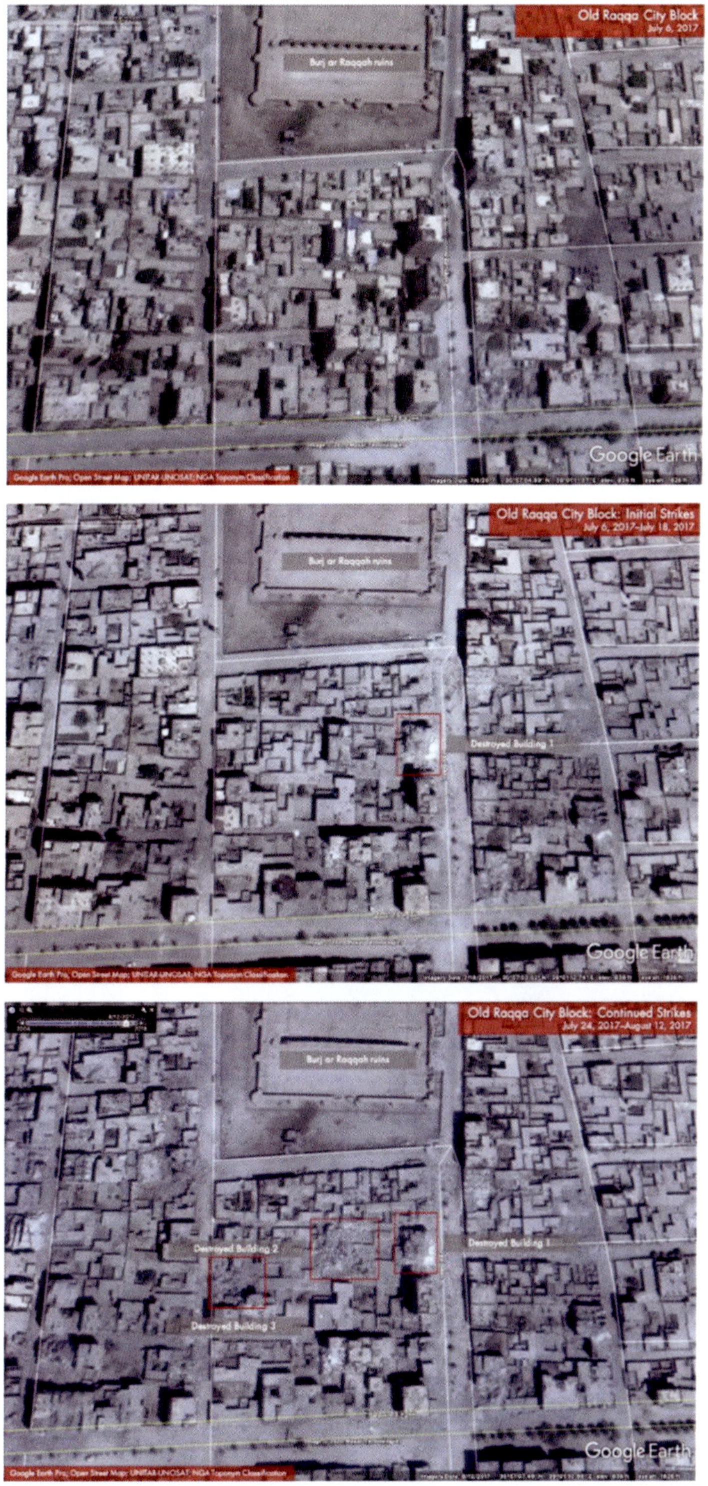

SOURCES: Google Earth Pro, Maxar Technologies; OpenStreetMap.

By the end of September 2017, coalition-backed SDF fighters drove remaining ISIS fighters into the 4 km^2 of Raqqa city centered around the al-Naim roundabout (Figure 3.4).[38] ISIS fighters took shelter in heavily fortified buildings, such as the Raqqa municipal hospital and state football stadium. In its entirety, this area comprised two and a half neighborhoods in north-central Raqqa. It was collectively referred to as the "circle of hell" for its reputation as being laden with ISIS-planted booby traps.[39] ISIS fighters hiding inside the building in this area did not appear to have a plan for how to leave.[40]

Battle for Raqqa: Securing Phase and Battle Assessment

By October 2017, several hundred ISIS fighters in Raqqa had withdrawn to defend 4 km^2 in the central and northern parts of Raqqa. As will be detailed in Chapter Four, civilian casualty incidents rose during the final few weeks of the Raqqa operation, even though the total amount of air and artillery strikes declined during that period. The most likely explanation for this outcome is that ISIS fighters were using civilians as human shields as they hunkered down to fight the SDF over the remaining neighborhoods under ISIS control. In this smaller area, ISIS fighters could monitor civilian movement and prevent the remaining civilians from escaping, using tactics that we describe further in Chapter Five. As we explore in greater detail in the next chapter, civilian casualty reports from this period support the theory: A review of the two civilian casualty incidents in October 2017 that CJTF-OIR assessed to be

Figure 3.4
The "Circle of Hell" in Raqqa Before and After the Operation

SOURCES: Google Earth Pro, Maxar Technologies; OpenStreetMap.

---

38 Dillon and Stump, 2017.

39 Quentin Sommerville and Riam Dalati, "The City Fit for No-One: Inside the Ruined 'Capital' of the Islamic State Group," BBC News, September 27, 2017a.

40 Sommerville and Dalati, 2017a.

"credible" (i.e., assessed as more likely than not to have been caused by coalition fires) found that both took place in the small area of Raqqa that remained under ISIS control during that time.[41] And, if the civilian casualty analysis also includes 14 civilian casualties in October 2017 that NGO investigations assessed with a high degree of confidence to be caused by coalition fires, 13 of the 14 casualties took place in the same tight battlespace under ISIS's control during that time.[42]

To avoid further civilian casualties and damage to downtown Raqqa, the city's tribal leaders and representatives from the local governing council began negotiating a deal with ISIS to end the fighting in Raqqa. The coalition did not support these negotiations. On October 13, 2017, BGen James Glynn, deputy commanding general of SOJTF-OIR, said that the coalition's "position is that we cannot agree with relocating Daesh fighters to create a problem elsewhere in this country."[43] Despite this stated position, the coalition did not block a deal brokered between the SDF and ISIS on October 15, 2017, specifying that ISIS would surrender Raqqa in exchange for safe passage out of the city. Publicly, the coalition reported that the deal was for Syrian and Iraqi ISIS fighters and their families.[44] However, one report found that ISIS evacuees included foreign ISIS fighters and their families. The report estimated that 4,000 people evacuated Raqqa as a result of the deal: 250 were ISIS fighters, 3,500 were ISIS family members, and the remaining were civilians forcibly removed from Raqqa by ISIS to be used as human shields.[45]

---

[41] CJTF-OIR, "CJTF-OIR Monthly Civilian Casualty Report," press release, October 27, 2017c.

[42] Amnesty International, undated.

[43] Feras Kilani, "Fall of Raqqa: IS Fighters Seeking a Deal to Move Safely out of the City," video, BBC News, October 13, 2017.

[44] Elizabeth McLaughlin, "100 ISIS Fighters Surrender in Raqqa in Sign That Battle to Retake the Syrian City Could Be Winding Down," ABC News, October 14, 2017.

[45] Sommerville and Dalati, 2017b.

CHAPTER FOUR

Civilian Harm in the Battle for Raqqa

In this chapter, we analyze the data available on civilian harm in Raqqa from June 2017 to October 2017, including civilian casualty estimates and building and infrastructure damage. Because of the limitations on civilian-harm data described in Chapter One, our conclusions here are tentative. There are, in particular, two key limitations to the data analyzed in this chapter: an attribution challenge, which means that it is difficult to determine the exact cause of building damage or civilian casualties, and a comparison challenge, which means that it is difficult to make claims about the level of civilian casualties or building damage in Raqqa when comparing them with casualties and damage from other operations in the region at approximately the same time.

Nevertheless, we believe that the body of evidence reviewed in this chapter points to two tentative conclusions. First, though significant, the ratio of civilian casualties to building damage and combatant casualties in Raqqa was lower than expected, given the ratio in comparable operations. This was the likely result of two interconnected factors. First, despite a coalition strategy to encircle ISIS that limited official humanitarian corridors and formal pauses in fighting, civilians were still able to leave Raqqa during the battle. We will review estimates on Raqqa's civilian population throughout the battle period and explore some ways in which the coalition and the SDF encouraged civilians to leave. Second, the battle focused on a smaller and smaller amount of territory as the operation wore on. With a declining number of civilians in the city and the ever-shrinking battlespace, there were fewer civilian casualty incidents in the latter half of the Raqqa operation. The rate of civilian casualty incidents remained low during this time despite higher rates of fire from coalition munitions.

Our second conclusion is that the Raqqa operation involved a significant amount of building and other infrastructure damage, which severely undermined the ability of civilians to rebuild their city with limited local resources and international support. The high rate of building damage was the result of a reliance on air and artillery fires to root out a dug-in enemy and protect the lives of friendly forces. However, the level of damage in Raqqa was at odds with CJTF-OIR's stated intent to hand the city over to the Raqqa Civilian Council and the Raqqa Internal Security Force to "provide local governance and security so the people of Raqqa can return to their lives as quickly as possible."[1] Broadly, the military's plan for capturing the city (military encirclement and months of intense fires) was at odds with the U.S. government's actions on post-conflict reconstruction. As we will discuss later, the United States failed to restore even some element of the basic essential services that existed prior to military opera-

[1] Stephen Townsend and Adrian Rankine-Galloway, "Department of Defense Press Briefing by General Townsend via Teleconference from Baghdad, Iraq," transcript, U.S. Department of Defense, August 31, 2017.

tions or to sufficiently respond to the urgent need to clear unexploded ordinance from Raqqa following the battle. Thus, local forces and governing bodies faced the challenge of managing Raqqa's reconstruction but lacked the ability or support to carry out this mission.

Civilian Casualties in Raqqa

As we described in our discussion of study methodology in Chapter One, civilian casualty estimates are notoriously difficult to accurately assess. In Raqqa, the U.S. military and NGO organizations provided differing estimates of the number of civilians who were killed or injured during the battle (Figure 4.1). In Chapter Ten, we discuss the potential causes of discrepancies between NGO and U.S. military civilian casualty assessments.

As of November 2020, CJTF-OIR assessed that coalition forces were, more likely than not, responsible for 38 incidents involving 240 civilian casualties (178 killed and 62 wounded).[2] The exact location for each of the civilian casualty incidents that CJTF-OIR assessed to be credible is available for viewing on a website hosted by Airwars, which uses the U.S. Military Grid Reference System shared with them by DoD.[3] A consortium of local Syrian and international NGOs led by Amnesty International and Airwars provided a different assessment.

Figure 4.1
Estimates of Civilian Casualties During the Battle for Raqqa

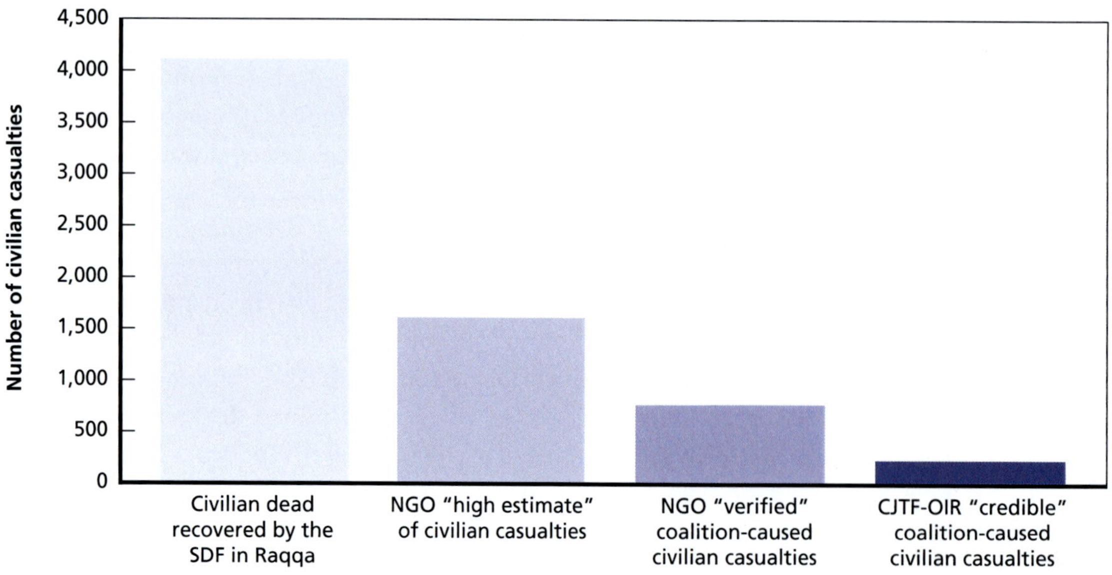

SOURCES: SDF Initial Response Team assessment of deceased civilians removed from Raqqa after the 2017 operation, which a Kurdish NGO worker shared with the authors in August 2020; Amnesty International, undated; CJTF-OIR, 2020.

---

2 See strike releases from June through October 2017, available from CJTF-OIR, undated.

3 The location of civilian casualty incidents assessed as credible claims during CJTF-OIR operations can be found via Airwars, "The Credibles," web tool, last updated March 13, 2020. These data include nearly all assessed civilian casualty incidents during the 2017 Raqqa operation.

The consortium conducted a study of Raqqa that included satellite imagery analysis, local and social media reporting, and three months of fieldwork.[4] That study presented several tiers of likelihood for civilian casualties that were the result of coalition military actions, and we examine two of those tiers for the sake of comparison.

The first tier—which is the third column in Figure 4.1, labeled as "verified" coalition-caused civilian casualties—includes 774 civilian casualties from 108 incidents (744 killed and 30 wounded). The NGO consortium was most confident in assessing that these verified casualties were the result of coalition actions; data on the verified casualties often include the name of the victim, the date and location of death, and the munition used in the strike. The second tier—the second column in the figure, labeled as "high estimate"—includes the approximately 1,600 civilian casualties that this consortium believes were the result of coalition action but could not find the same types of information as in the first tier to verify that conclusion.

The civilian casualty data compiled by the NGO consortium and the U.S. military include only the civilians who were assessed to be killed or injured by coalition forces. However, to fully understand the extent of civilian harm during the operation, we need to know the total number of civilian casualties. Through a Kurdish NGO worker based in northeastern Syria, we acquired SDF data on the total number of bodies uncovered from the rubble during and after the Raqqa operation. As of November 2020, the SDF estimated that it uncovered 4,118 dead civilians in Raqqa during the operation and an additional 1,878 people who appeared to be dressed in military gear. Although this number likely helps us understand the number of civilians killed in Raqqa, it does not help us understand the extent to which any other actor (e.g., ISIS) caused the deaths.

Building and Infrastructure Damage in Raqqa

Satellite imagery analysis conducted in the aftermath of the battle showed that the level of structural damage in Raqqa was unparalleled in the counter-ISIS war effort. According to the United Nations Institute for Training and Research, approximately 11,000 buildings were either damaged or destroyed in Raqqa between February and October 2017—corresponding to approximately 40 buildings destroyed per day.[5] SGM John Wayne Troxell, senior enlisted adviser to Chairman of the Joint Chiefs of Staff Dunford, described the artillery effort against ISIS in Raqqa as follows: "Every minute of every hour we were putting some kind of fire on ISIS in Raqqa."[6] In fact, USMC artillery batteries deployed to the outskirts of Raqqa burned out two Howitzer guns during the battle.[7] "I've never heard of it," explained a former Army artillery officer to the *Military Times*. "Normally your gun goes back to depot for full reset well before that happens."[8] Another former Marine interviewed for this study remarked,

---

4 Amnesty International, undated.

5 United Nations Institute for Training and Research, 2017.

6 Luke Mogelson, "America's Abandonment of Syria," *New Yorker,* April 20, 2020.

7 Mogelson, 2020.

8 Shawn Snow, "Marine Artillery Barrage of Raqqa Was So Intense Two Howitzers Burned Out," *Marine Corps Times,* November 2, 2017.

"I was involved in the 2004 Fallujah offensive, and Raqqa far exceeds the destruction in Fallujah in 2004."[9]

As shown in Figure 4.2, the highest rate of building damage density occurred in the central neighborhoods of the city. An international NGO estimated, using United Nations satellite imagery, that 12–15 buildings were damaged or destroyed per hectare (about 2.5 acres) in the central neighborhoods of Raqqa. However, the amount of structural damage was lower in the city outskirts, which were the least dense and earliest captured parts of Raqqa. The neighborhoods on Raqqa's outskirts still sustained significant damage but at rates three to five times lower than in the center of the city (one to four buildings damaged per hectare in the outskirts).[10]

Raqqa also suffered enormous damage to economically and culturally significant infrastructure, including bridges, marketplaces, and community service locations. For example, among the destroyed buildings were eight hospitals, 29 mosques, more than 40 schools, and five universities, and the city's water irrigation systems were also destroyed.[11] Damage to key facilities followed the general pattern of damage density in Raqqa described earlier and shown

Figure 4.2
Damage Analysis After the Battle for Raqqa

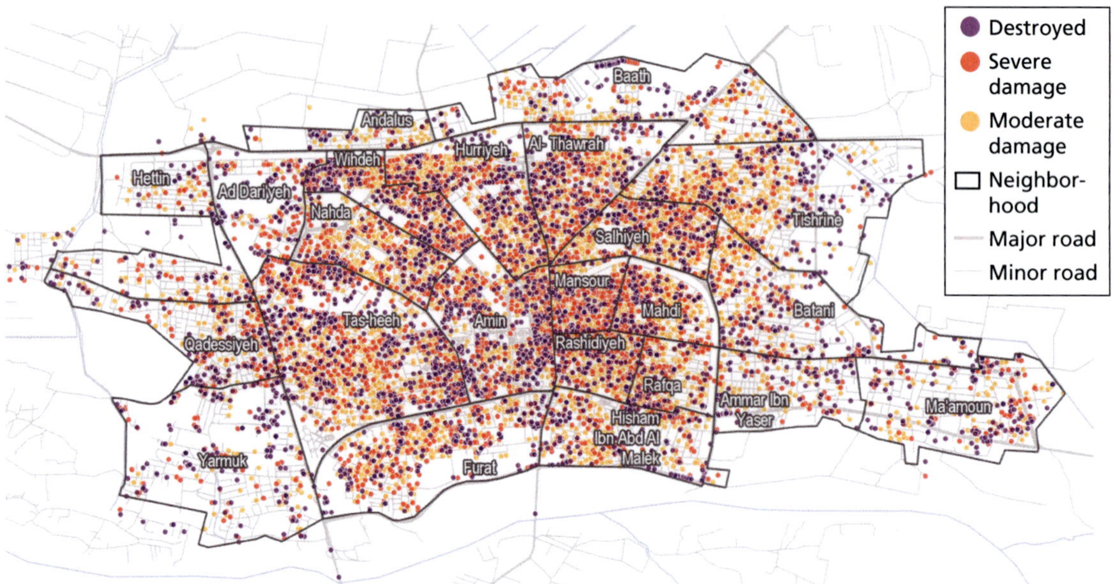

SOURCE: REACH Initiative, 2019, p. 13.
NOTE: The points on the map of Raqqa correspond to structures assessed as being damaged or destroyed between February 3 and October 23, 2017.

[9] Former U.S. Marine who worked on the humanitarian response during the Raqqa operation, interview with the authors, August 2020.

[10] REACH Initiative, *Syrian Cities Damage Atlas—Eight Year Anniversary of the Syrian Civil War: Thematic Assessment of Satellite Identified Damage*, Geneva, March 16, 2019.

[11] Roos Boer, Laurie Treffers, and Chris Woods, *Seeing Through the Rubble: The Civilian Impact of the Use of Explosive Weapons in the Fight Against ISIS*, Airwars and Pax, October 2020, p. 30.

in Figure 4.2. An NGO's critical services assessment conducted at the start of 2018 found that residents in the central neighborhoods in the city often had to travel to neighborhoods in the outskirts of the city to find drinkable water, health care, basic foodstuffs, and education.[12]

Insufficient Post-Battle Reconstruction Efforts

Despite the extensive damage to civilian structures and infrastructure caused by the coalition's military operations, the U.S. government did not marshal the resources needed to assist local actors in Raqqa with the reconstruction of the city. For example, the most urgent need following the fighting was to clear the explosive remnants of war in and around Raqqa so that civilians could return home safely and humanitarian actors, NGOs, and commercial suppliers could enter the area to begin the process of reconstruction. Field work in Raqqa by the NGO Human Rights Watch found that, between October 21, 2017, and January 20, 2018, mines injured at least 491 people, including 157 children, many of whom died.[13] According to State Department officials involved in the post-reconstruction effort in Raqqa, the Department of State, USAID, and DoD did prioritize the clearing of explosive remnants of war early, but their effort underestimated the level of those remnants in the city, and resourcing, staff, and funds ultimately fell short.[14]

Moreover, the U.S. government's effort to provide and restore basic essential services, such as clearing rubble, fixing water and electricity systems, and repairing bridges, also fell short.[15] According to one United Nations official, "There was bewilderment among the humanitarian community and even many of the SOJTF staff as to how things proceeded after the offensive was over. We hit a huge cliff post-combat operations with the stabilization effort. Much of it was connected to the lack of appetite to resource it and policy-related uncertainty as to how long [the United States] would stay engaged in Syria."[16] Despite public pronouncements from the CENTCOM commander and USAID administrator about the importance of the reconstruction effort in Raqqa,[17] the White House suspended stabilization aid to Syria in March 2018.[18] According to one State Department official, the suspension of recovery assistance had

> an inordinate and devastating impact on efforts by START [the Syria Transition Assistance Response Team], SSAP [USAID's Southern Syria Assistance Platform], and other development actors and implementers receiving funding from the U.S. government for the purposes of stabilizing Raqqa. Cutting funding mid-stream, ending long-term agreements,

---

12 REACH Initiative, 2018.

13 Human Rights Watch, "Syria: Landmines Kill, Injure Hundreds in Raqqa," February 12, 2018.

14 State Department officials, interview with the authors, October 2020.

15 State Department officials, interview with the authors, October 2020.

16 UN official, interview with the authors, August 2020.

17 U.S. Agency for International Development, "On the Record Interview with USAID Administrator Mark Green and Commander of US Central Command Joseph Votel, Al-Raqqa Province, Syria," press release, January 22, 2018.

18 Eric Schmitt, Helene Cooper, and Alissa J. Rubin, "Trump Orders State Dept. to Suspend Funds for Syria Recovery," *New York Times*, March 30, 2018.

and failing to restore some element of the basic essential services that existed—which were in large part destroyed due to U.S./coalition military action—is a large blemish accompanying the U.S. government's involvement in Syria.[19]

Civilian Harm in the Raqqa Operation in Context

Raqqa incurred the most damage density of any city in Syria during the civil war,[20] and there were almost 2,000 more structures damaged or destroyed there than in Mosul (9,225 structures), despite being one-fifth of Mosul's size by population (Raqqa's pre-operation population was about 300,000 and Mosul's population before operations started there in October 2016 was about 1.5 million).[21] In its strike releases from October 2016 to October 2017, CJTF-OIR reported slightly more targets in Mosul than in Raqqa (11,332 in Mosul; 10,605 in Raqqa).[22] But these targets were spread out over a longer period in Mosul, which is a much larger city. In Figure 4.3, we estimate the munitions used from CJTF-OIR's reported targets (for a detailed discussion of this estimation, see the methodology section in Chapter One). In Raqqa, there was a higher number of munitions per day over a shorter period at the height of the battle than there was in Mosul, suggesting that the Raqqa operation was shorter but more intense, especially considering how much smaller Raqqa's population is than Mosul's.[23]

One of the reasons for the different distributions of munition use between Mosul and Raqqa may be the cities' layouts. For example, General Townsend stated that "Mosul has got some big buildings, but they are spread out over the city." In Raqqa, by contrast, "there are a cluster of tall, dominant type of buildings. They are hard [to capture] for any army on the planet."[24] Some officials we interviewed noted that the most-intense damage in Raqqa was largely concentrated in specific neighborhoods.[25] This is true, but overall assessments found that Raqqa's outskirts were also damaged, despite being secured by coalition forces earliest in the operation. Overall, local organizations have estimated that 65 percent of homes in Raqqa

19 State Department official, interview with the authors, October 2020.

20 Ameen Najjar, "Damage Caused by the Syrian Civil War: What the Data Say," Towards Data Science, June 27, 2018.

21 Office of the United Nations High Commissioner for Refugees, "Iraq Situation: UNHCR Flash Update," Geneva, July 14, 2017; R. Lafta, V. Cetorelli, and G. Burnham, "Living in Mosul During the Time of ISIS and the Military Liberation: Results from a 40-Cluster Household Survey," *Conflict and Health*, Vol. 12, 2018, article 31; and Mariya Petkova, "What Will Happen to Post-ISIL Raqqa," Al Jazeera, October 17, 2017.

22 See strike releases for October 1, 2016, through October 31, 2017, available from CJTF-OIR, undated.

23 We acknowledge later in the chapter that the Iraqi Security Forces used artillery fires and air strikes in Mosul, which are not reflected in the CJTF-OIR strike releases, whereas all of the air strikes and artillery fires in Raqqa were conducted by the coalition. Moreover, we acknowledged in Chapter One that CJTF-OIR strike releases did not begin to include dynamic artillery strikes until April 21, 2017. Both factors would likely, on balance, increase the number of munitions used in Mosul from the ones shown in Figure 4.3. However, these missing munitions would not increase the number of munitions by a factor of five in Mosul, which is what they would need to do for munition use in Mosul to be proportional to the amount of munitions used in Raqqa.

24 Michael R. Gordon, "U.S.-Backed Forces Close to Trapping ISIS Holdouts in Raqqa," *New York Times*, July 2, 2017b.

25 Staff from NGOs reporting civilian casualties, interview with the authors, December 13, 2019.

Figure 4.3
Air and Artillery Munitions Employed in Raqqa and Mosul Operations

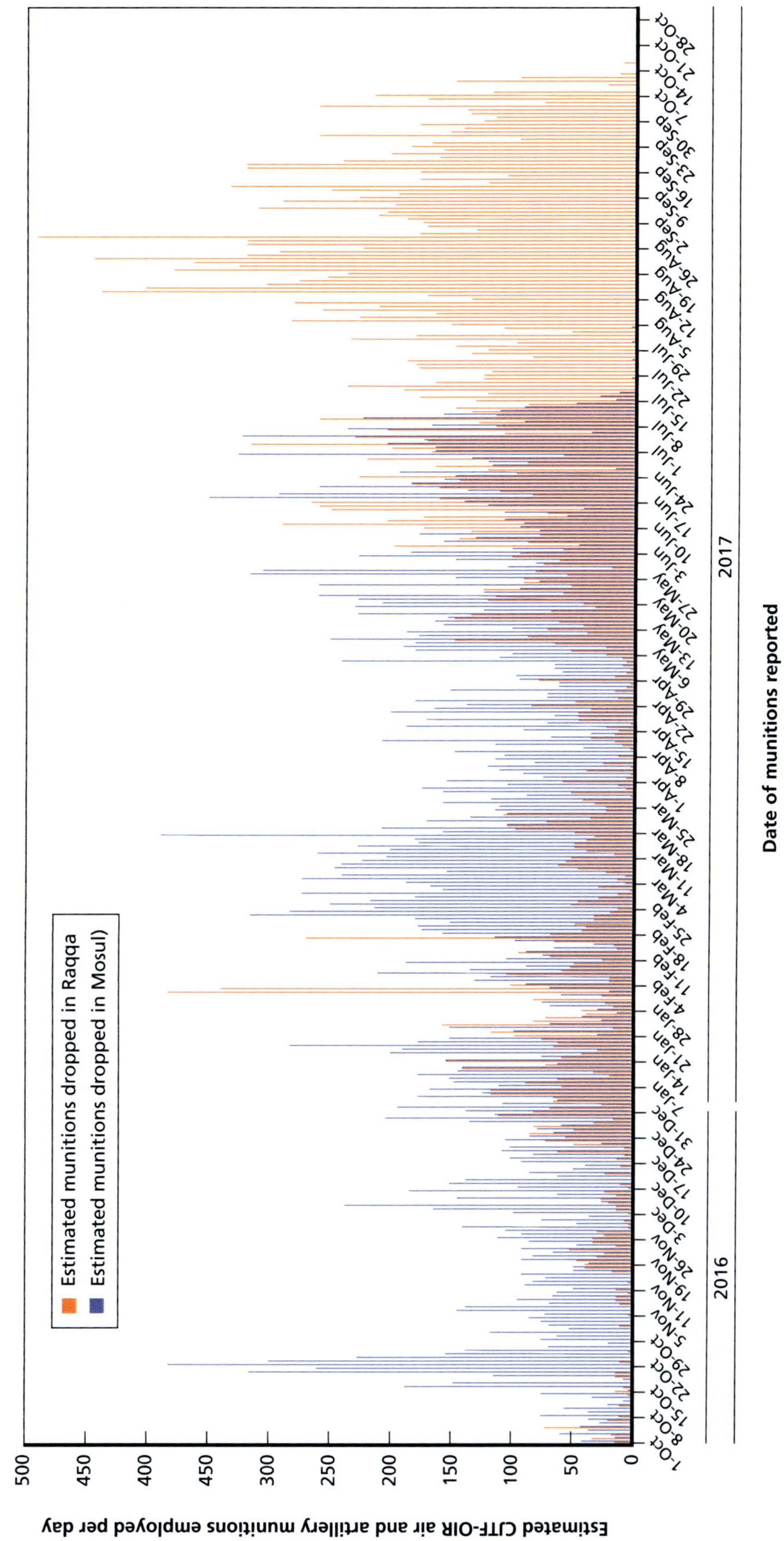

SOURCE: CJTF-OIR, undated.
NOTE: This graph shows the average estimated number of munitions derived from CJTF-OIR targets. There are, on average, three munitions per target.

were destroyed, and the United Nations Office for the Coordination of Humanitarian Affairs claimed that 80 percent of the city was rendered "uninhabitable."[26]

A second complicating factor is that damage assessments do not differentiate between damage caused by ISIS and damage caused by coalition fires (see Chapter Five for more information on ISIS defensive tactics). In Mosul, ISIS was responsible for more improvised explosive devices than in Raqqa, so a greater proportion of the damage in Raqqa was likely caused by coalition fires.[27]

A third complicating factor when comparing Mosul and Raqqa is the source of fires. In Raqqa, the coalition controlled all air or ground strikes. In Mosul, Iraqi forces also conducted air and artillery strikes, coordinating and deconflicting with coalition force strikes. As one general officer noted, there were days when a single Iraqi Corps launched more than 1,000 artillery pieces into ISIS areas, causing significant cumulative damage in Mosul.[28] Thus, simply comparing coalition-dropped fires for both cities might not provide a full picture.

Nevertheless, the level of damage during the campaign to retake Raqqa was significant. It prompted many Raqqa residents, activists, and members of the city's civilian governing infrastructure to resent the coalition's approach to liberating the city. One activist put it this way: "The shelling before was for specific places. Now it's just randomly shelling."[29] Local frustrations with the level of building damage during the operation grew larger after the city was captured from ISIS because of the minimal funding set aside for the reconstruction of Raqqa.

Despite the high level of building damage, the number of civilians who died in Raqqa was lower than expected, given the ratio of buildings damaged or destroyed to civilian casualties in Mosul and Aleppo (Figure 4.4). This suggests, though by no means proves, that targeting in Raqqa—the vast majority of which was conducted by U.S. forces—was more precise in its targeting and in avoiding civilian loss of life, even though that loss was extensive. During the battle for Mosul, there were 9,000–11,000 civilians killed and approximately 9,925 structures damaged or destroyed.[30] Although we did not analyze the degree to which the Iraqi Security Forces might have been responsible for civilian harm, those forces played a far larger role providing supporting fires in Mosul than the lightly armed SDF played in Raqqa.

For a second comparison between cities, the battle for Aleppo was fought from 2012 to 2016 between the Syrian government and various anti-government forces. An estimated 31,250 civilians were killed and 35,691 structures damaged or destroyed during the fighting.[31] In Mosul and Aleppo, the ratio of buildings destroyed or damaged to civilians killed was

---

[26] "Amnesty International Says US-Led Coalition Destroyed Syria's Raqqa," France 24, May 6, 2018; United Nations Office for the Coordination of Humanitarian Affairs, "Syria Crisis: Northeast Syria Situation Report No. 16 (1–30 September 2017)," October 19, 2017; and Mark Lowcock, "Briefing to the Security Council on the Humanitarian Situation in Raqqa and Rukban," United Nations Office for the Coordination of Humanitarian Affairs, April 17, 2018.

[27] Boer, Treffers, and Woods, 2020.

[28] General officer, interview with the authors, September 2020.

[29] Sophie McNeill, "Raqqa: Monitoring Groups Sound Alarm over Civilian Death Toll as Islamic State Fight Heats Up," Australian Broadcasting Corporation, June 27, 2017.

[30] Office of the United Nations High Commissioner for Refugees, 2017; and Susannah George, Qassim Abdul-Zahra, Maggie Michael, and Lori Hinnant, "Mosul Is a Graveyard: Final IS Battle Kills 9,000 Civilians," Associated Press, December 20, 2017.

[31] Najjar, 2018; and Violations Documentation Center in Syria, "Civilian Casualties in Aleppo," web tool, undated, data sorted from July 19, 2012, until December 22, 2016.

Figure 4.4
Structural Damage and Civilian Casualty Figures in Raqqa, Mosul, and Aleppo

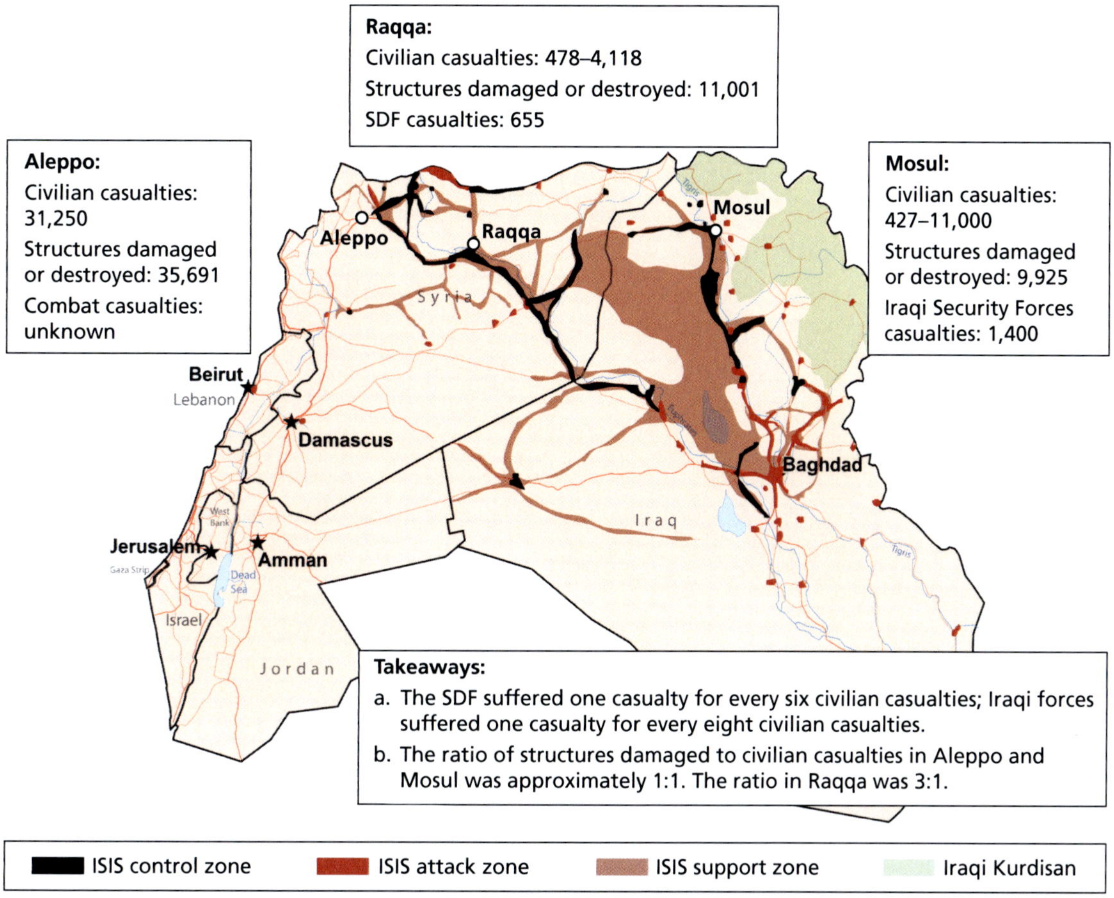

SOURCES: Base image: Institute for the Study of War, "ISIS Sanctuary: August 8, 2014," map, August 4, 2015; used with permission. Aleppo building damage estimates: Najjar, 2018. Aleppo civilian casualty estimates: Violations Documentation Center in Syria, undated, data pulled for July 19, 2012, until December 22, 2016. Aleppo combatant deaths: not available. Raqqa building damage estimates: Najjar, 2018; Raqqa civilian casualties: Amnesty International, undated. Raqqa combatant casualties (for the SDF): Louisa Loveluck, "U.S.-Led Coalition Declares ISIS Forces Vanquished, Battle for Raqqa Over," *Washington Post*, October 20, 2017. Mosul building damage estimates: Office of the United Nations High Commissioner for Refugees, 2017. Mosul civilian casualties: George et al., 2017. Mosul combatant casualties (for the Iraqi Security Forces): Helene Cooper, "Revived After Mosul, Iraqi Forces Prepare to Battle ISIS in Tal Afar," *New York Times*, August 18, 2017.

NOTE: Comparisons between civilian casualties and combatant casualties or building damage shown in the takeaways rely on the highest reliable estimate of civilian casualties for each city. In Aleppo, this was 31,250 civilians killed; in Raqqa, it was 4,118; and in Mosul, it was 11,000. Low-end estimates show the civilians killed in Raqqa and Mosul as assessed by CJTF-OIR.

approximately 1:1. In Raqqa, there were an estimated 11,000 structures damaged or destroyed, and the SDF estimated that it removed 4,118 dead civilians in Raqqa after the 2017 operation.[32] Assuming that the deceased civilians recovered by the SDF died during the Raqqa operation, and setting aside the likelihood that some were executed for reasons having nothing to do with the rate of fires, the ratio of buildings destroyed to civilians killed in Raqqa was 3:1.

[32] For estimates of civilian casualties in Raqqa, see Amnesty International, undated.

In addition to comparing the extent of structural damage between Mosul and Raqqa, we can compare casualties of friendly forces. The SDF reported that 655 of its soldiers died in the fight to capture Raqqa.[33] Compared with the SDF's estimate that it found 4,118 civilian dead in Raqqa (see Figure 4.1), this meant that the SDF lost approximately one combatant per six civilians killed in Raqqa. In comparison, approximately 1,400 members of the Iraqi Security Forces were killed during the fight to liberate Mosul from ISIS control.[34] The Associated Press estimated that 11,000 civilians died during the operation, which means that the Iraqi Security Forces lost approximately one combatant per eight civilian casualties. This suggests that, although the SDF received more close air and artillery support during the operation because of its lack of organic fires, the operation to capture Raqqa from ISIS involved substantial risk, and SDF fighters were still putting themselves in harm's way.

Taken together, there were three times fewer civilian casualties in Raqqa than buildings damaged, and there were more combatant casualties of SDF fighters per civilian casualty in Raqqa than in Mosul. These findings are not definitive, but they do suggest that civilian harm in Raqqa, while significant, was lower than in other operations in the same region around the same time.

In addition, the number of civilian casualty incidents in Raqqa was lower than what might otherwise be expected given the rate of fires during the operation. The graph in Figure 4.5 shows that civilian casualty incidents were concentrated in the first half of the operation and tapered off by the second half, even though munitions employed by the coalition increased. What is evident in the figure is that a rise in munitions used during the Raqqa operation did not necessarily correspond with a rise in civilian casualty incidents. One factor that might explain this is the shrinking size of the battlespace in Raqqa, as shown in the battle progression map in Chapter Three (Figure 3.2). ISIS controlled fewer neighborhoods in Raqqa by late September 2017, and thus fewer civilians could be put in harm's way. A second potential explanation for why civilian casualties were unrelated to munition use (and building damage) is that the number of civilians in the city declined over time. We explore this second factor next.

Civilian Departures and Evacuation from Raqqa

Raqqa's civilian population declined steadily during the operation. An NGO estimated that the civilian population in Raqqa declined from an estimated 269,000 in April 2017 to as few as 2,000 to 3,000 civilians by the end of the fighting in October 2017. As shown in Figure 4.5, the sharpest decline in civilian population during the battle occurred around the same time as the breaching of the Old City walls on July 4, 2017. The NGO estimated that, on June 23, 2017, 100,000–150,000 civilians remained in Raqqa; on July 6, that estimate declined to 20,000–50,000. And the NGO estimated that, on August 18, approximately one week after

33 People's Defense Units, 2017.

34 Cooper, 2017.

Figure 4.5
Civilian Casualty Incidents and Number of Targets Struck in Raqqa per Day of the Operation

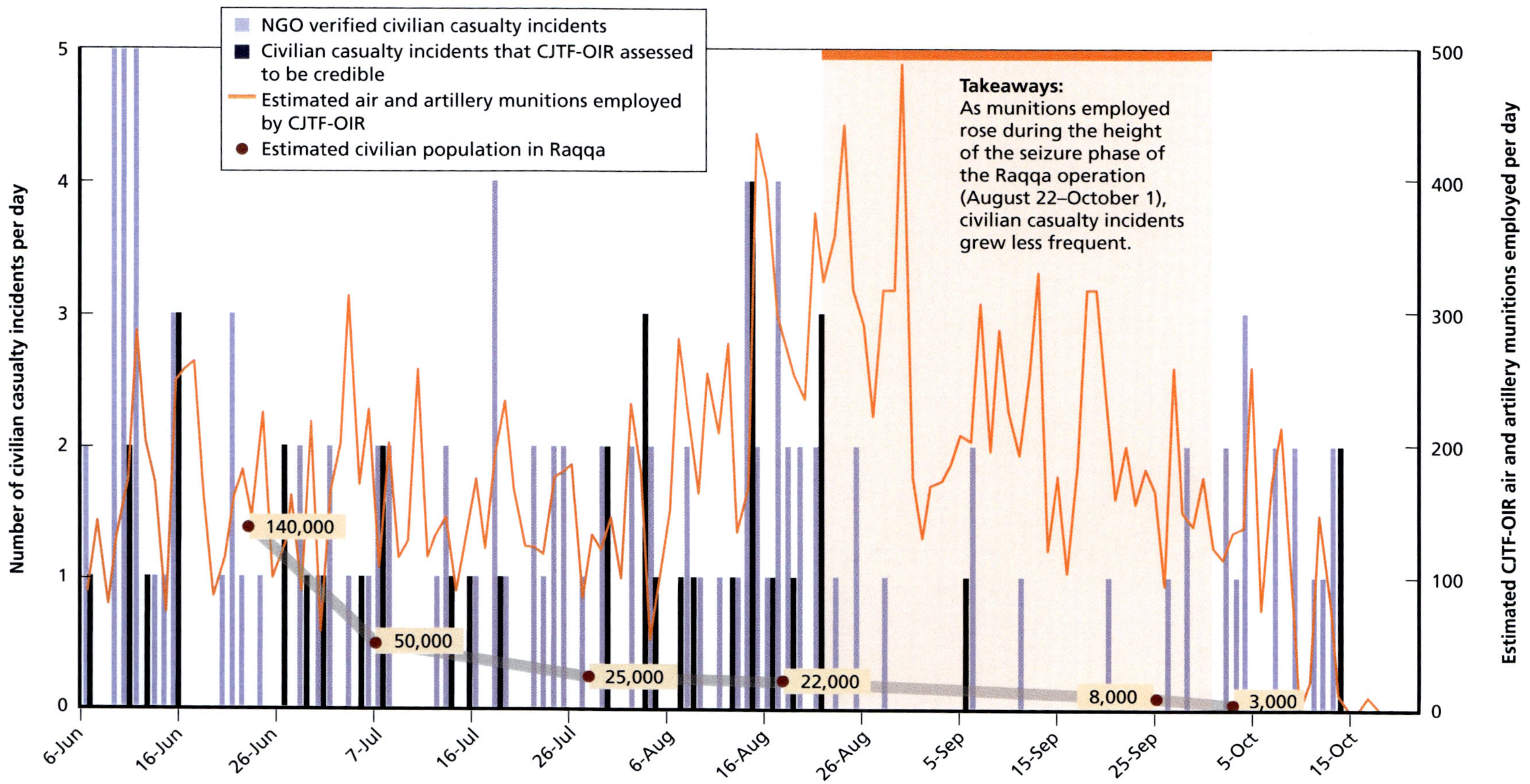

SOURCES: CJTF-OIR, undated; Airwars-compiled data shared with the authors; Amnesty International, undated; REACH Initiative, 2017; and Situation Overviews I–V, available at ReliefWeb, "Ar-Raqqa City, Syria—Situation Overview, 13 October 2017," webpage, October 13, 2017 (dates June 23, July 6, July 28, August 17, and September 25).

the halfway point of the operation and roughly at the start of the most-intense bombardment, the civilian population of Raqqa was approximately 22,000 people.[35] That number represents only about 8 percent of the pre-battle population, but it meant that a significant number of civilians were still at risk.

In general, deliberate efforts to draw the civilian population out of a city in advance of fighting are critical for three reasons: to reduce the incidence of civilian casualties; to deny enemy fighters the opportunity to hide among noncombatant populations, which helps increase the effectiveness of precision targeting; and to draw out enemy forces into the open so that they can be positively identified and attacked.[36] The coalition's chosen strategy of encircling and defeating ISIS in Raqqa meant that coalition forces did not implement any formal pauses or negotiate exit corridors that might have allowed civilians (and potentially ISIS fighters) to leave the city prior to and during the fighting. Nevertheless, according to the NGO data represented in Figure 4.5, civilians did appear to have departed Raqqa during the battle—despite ISIS efforts to retain them as human shields (ISIS's tactics to prevent civilians from leaving Raqqa are discussed in greater detail in Chapter Five) and despite the lack of formal pauses or exit corridors.

U.S. ground forces and the SDF also took some steps to encourage civilians to leave the city. For example, prior to the assault on Raqqa, coalition pilots dropped leaflets warning civilians that the operation was about to begin. The leaflets instructed civilians to leave the city and stay away from ISIS to the extent possible.[37] During the operation, the coalition continued to use leaflets to send messages to the civilian population, including communicating desired behaviors for identifying themselves as noncombatants seeking to escape the city.[38] The monitoring group Raqqa Is Being Slaughtered Silently uploaded two such examples of these leaflets: One told residents to use the document as they sought refuge with SDF soldiers, and another instructed civilians to approach an SDF soldier with a strip of something white.[39] U.S. ground forces also employed information operations to remove civilians from the city to reduce resistance and civilian casualties.[40] According to U.S. SOF operating in Raqqa, throughout the operation, U.S. forces utilized a variety of nonkinetic shaping measures directed at Raqqa's civilian population. These measures were designed to undermine civilian support for ISIS by exposing the group's atrocities, instruct civilians on safe passage, separate civilians from ISIS, and highlight SDF efforts to protect the local population.[41] For example, U.S. forces assisted the SDF with the development of radio stations, which were useful in helping the U.S. and coalition forces gain the upper hand in the civilian harm "blame game."[42]

---

[35] REACH Initiative, 2017. Also includes data on civilian population estimates in Raqqa from Situation Overviews I–V, available from ReliefWeb, 2017.

[36] Former U.S. military tactical ground unit commander, interview with the authors, April 2020; and John R. Ballard, "Lessons Learned from Operation *AL FAJR*: The Liberation of Fallujah," 10th Annual Command and Control Research and Technology Symposium: The Future of C2, Washington, D.C., 2005.

[37] Field grade military officer, email correspondence with the authors, November 2020.

[38] Field grade military officer, email correspondence with the authors, November 2020.

[39] Raqqa Is Being Slaughtered Silently, Facebook post, May 28, 2017.

[40] Cynthia Innocenti, "Shaping the Information War: Military Information Combats Propaganda," U.S. Central Command, April 11, 2017.

[41] Field grade military officer, email correspondence with the authors, November 2020.

[42] U.S. military tactical ground unit operator, interview with the authors, May 2020.

Furthermore, the SDF took some steps of its own to help remove civilians from the city.[43] According to a Kurdish activist who observed the Raqqa operation, the SDF formed special "rescue teams" to engage tribal elders, local notables, and the Raqqa Civil Council before and during military operations in Raqqa to communicate about forthcoming attacks and help civilians escape.[44] When civilians left the city, they would gather at collection points before transferring to the Ain Issa refugee camp. At these refugee camps, an SDF unit interviewed civilians about the situation in Raqqa, including the civilian picture.[45] Throughout the offensive, the SDF attempted to maintain contact with local civilian leaders. Military officials involved in the Raqqa operation observed that the SDF played a role in protecting civilians in Raqqa, including facilitating the evacuation of civilians from the city.[46] As civilians escaped ISIS-controlled areas, they were met with assistance by the SDF. According to one U.S. SOF operator, the coalition had to delay operations several times because the SDF gave away food and water meant for their troops to civilians trying to escape the city.[47] One general officer noted, "As Raqqa progressed, the Arab component of the SDF was interacting and intervening in the operations to try to slow things down and force discussions and negotiations with ISIS, local sheiks, and others."[48] These discussions eventually led to the negotiated exit for ISIS fighters in October 2017, described in the previous chapter, which ultimately ended the battle. The coalition did not approve of the negotiated exit. According to a U.S. ground operator in Raqqa, "ISIS of course would and did take advantage of [the negotiated exit], but Gen. Mazloum [Abdi] was under pressure from the Raqqa Civil Council to negotiate an exit path to limit the amount of harm to civilians still trapped in the city."[49]

In sum, coalition forces and the SDF took important steps to remove civilians from Raqqa prior to and during combat operations. Civilians were able to leave the city, as evidenced by the aforementioned population estimates, despite the coalition's overall strategy of encircling and destroying ISIS in Raqqa. Still, any civilians who did flee the city in response to leaflet drops or information from the coalition were not permitted to do so within the safety of a formal exit corridor or pause. Although the exit corridor ultimately negotiated to end the battle likely reduced additional civilian harm, it was not something that was planned in advance or approved by the coalition. Moreover, although it is important to evacuate civilians in advance of seizing a city, it is also critically important to resettle civilians once combat ends. Civilian displacement is another form of civilian harm, and because of the extensive battle destruction and inadequate post-conflict resource investments, many of the civilians forced to flee from Raqqa likely became refugees or internally displaced persons.

---

[43] According to a CJTF-OIR spokesman, "The SDF have encouraged civilians to depart Raqqa so that they do not become trapped, used as human shields or targets for ISIS snipers" (CJTF-OIR, "SDF Begins Raqqa Offensive, Progress Continues in Mosul," press release, June 6, 2017a).

[44] Kurdish activist, interview with the authors, July 2020.

[45] Humanitarian worker in northeast Syria, interview with the authors, July 2020.

[46] General officer, interview with the authors, July 2020; U.S. SOF operator, interview with the authors, January 2021.

[47] U.S. SOF operator, interview with the authors, January 2021.

[48] General officer, interview with the authors, July 2020.

[49] U.S. SOF operator, interview with the authors, July 2020.

CHAPTER FIVE

The Contribution of ISIS Defensive Tactics to Civilian Harm in Raqqa

CJTF-OIR had long publicly stated its objective of removing ISIS from Raqqa, so the group had years to prepare its defenses of the city.[1] In the six months leading up to the battle for Raqqa, CJTF-OIR assessed that ISIS had anywhere between 2,000 and 4,000 local and foreign fighters in the city, plus 900–1,600 in the surrounding countryside.[2] CJTF-OIR knew that ISIS was a hybrid fighting force that employed more-conventional fighting tactics until it was clear that its fighters were about to be overwhelmed. At that point, ISIS would shift to terrorist and unconventional tactics to leverage its limited resources and attrit opposing forces. The coalition expected ISIS to make a last stand in Raqqa, a culmination of the coalition's fight to eliminate the physical caliphate and remove its presence from the second capital city.[3] In advance of the fight in Raqqa, U.S. forces observed ISIS's approach to fighting during the battle for Mosul, where ISIS used many of the same defensive mechanisms, including using civilians as human shields, booby traps, snipers, tunnels, and improvised explosive devices.[4]

In this chapter, we explore ISIS's defensive tactics in Raqqa, which posed significant challenges to U.S. and coalition ground forces attempting to mitigate civilian harm during the operation. We describe how ISIS used civilians and civilian infrastructure in Raqqa, making it extremely difficult for coalition forces to isolate combatants from the civilian population.

During the battle for Raqqa, ISIS forced SDF fighters on the ground into building-by-building urban warfare through a complex, sophisticated network of (1) hardened militants, including snipers and suicide bombers, and (2) tactics, including mines, improvised explosive devices, and tunnels that crisscrossed the city. ISIS "used hospitals, mosques, schools and otherwise-protected sites for the planning, execution and support of [its] military operations," in direct violation of international law.[5] The group also deliberately developed a complex operational military structure across military, civilian, and "dual-use institutions that simultaneously perform[ed] military and civilian functions," in order to hamper the ability of the SDF

[1] Senior military officials, interview with the authors, July 2020.

[2] Kogan, 2017, p. 38; Dorrian, 2017c.

[3] National Counterterrorism Center intelligence analysts, interview with the authors, January 2020. However, although ISIS fighters fought hard to keep the city, it was not the group's final stand. The final battle occurred in the town of Baghouz, Syria, in 2019 (retired senior military officer, interview with the authors, July 2020).

[4] John Dorrian, "Department of Defense Press Briefing by Col. Dorrian via teleconference from Baghdad, Iraq," transcript, U.S. Department of Defense, April 12, 2017a.

[5] CENTCOM, "Syrian Democratic Forces Liberate Raqqah," press release, No. 17-409, October 20, 2017.

and U.S.-led coalition forces to distinguish ISIS fighters from civilians.[6] For example, multiple DoD and NGO sources acknowledged that ISIS turned Raqqa's national hospital into a multi-use headquarters military facility and trapped civilians inside.[7] ISIS routinely used doctors, nurses, and patients as human shields.

According to Raqqa residents, ISIS kept local populations "like rats in a cage" and deliberately employed tactics that would significantly hinder the ability of coalition forces to isolate combatants from the broader population.[8] Our interviews with multiple U.S. military officials highlighted how ISIS exploited knowledge of U.S. ROE and commitment to civilian protection to evade targeting by coalition forces and the SDF.[9] For more geospatial intelligence analysis on how ISIS repurposed civilian buildings and their targeting by coalition air strikes, see Section Five of the online annex.

ISIS militants converted entire neighborhoods into networked fortresses, removing any distinction between protected buildings and legitimate targets and moving rapidly among buildings, bunkers, and tunnels. ISIS fighters covered commercial streets with long canopies and broke holes into the walls of adjacent homes to conceal their movements from coalition surveillance assets in the sky.[10] As a U.S. Army armor officer wrote in 2018, ISIS's approach negated the promise of precision-strike capability, leaving civilians "facing a future little different than if they had been hammered with dumb bombs and indiscriminate artillery salvos."[11] In Raqqa, the group maintained a primitive chemical weapon capability and used unmanned aerial systems (UAS) for reconnaissance and air strikes against the SDF and coalition forces. ISIS also increased its usage of house-borne improvised explosive devices in Raqqa, which were rigged to collapse on SDF fighters.

Furthermore, ISIS deliberately prevented civilians from leaving Raqqa. ISIS snipers were dispersed throughout the city to shoot any civilians who tried to escape, and the group forcibly relocated civilians to areas near or behind its front lines as the offensive progressed. ISIS used suicide bombers who blew themselves up in groups of civilians who tried to leave Raqqa. According to a Kurdish activist in Raqqa at the time, fighters were "camouflaging themselves in civilian clothes, sending suicide bombers out among civilians trying to flee through safe passages that we were preparing. These bombers would . . . send a message of intimidation to civilians—'if you go out [try to leave Raqqa], you will be killed.'"[12] Moreover, according to our

---

[6] ISIS established "observational equivalence between [civilian] victims and [ISIS] supporters" (Mara R. Revkin, "When Terrorists Govern: Protecting Civilians in Conflicts with State-Building Armed Groups," *Harvard National Security Journal*, Vol. 9, 2018, p. 101). See also Raqqah Study Group, 2018, pp. 12–13.

[7] Airwars, "U.S.-Led Coalition in Iraq & Syria: Airwars Assessment," incident CS1643, October 17, 2017; David Sim, "Battle for Raqqa Photos: ISIS Confined to Hospital and Stadium, with Hostages and Snipers in Both," *International Business Times*, October 3, 2017; Maher Al-Hamdan, "The Ongoing Medical Crisis in Raqqa," Atlantic Council, May 16, 2018; and Ryan Dillon and Adrian Rankine-Galloway, "Department of Defense Press Briefing by Colonel Dillon via Teleconference from Baghdad, Iraq," transcript, U.S. Department of Defense, September 21, 2017.

[8] Amnesty International, 2017, p. 23.

[9] Senior military officials and a retired senior military official, interview with the authors, July 2020.

[10] Kogan, 2017, p. 38; and John Dorrian, "Department of Defense Press Briefing by Col. Dorrian via Teleconference from Baghdad, Iraq," transcript, April 26, 2017b.

[11] Amos C. Fox, "Precision Fires Hindered by Urban Jungle," Association of the United States Army, April 16, 2018.

[12] Kurdish civilian activist who was a direct observer in the battle, interview with the authors, July 1, 2020.

interviews with those familiar with the negotiations between Raqqa tribal leaders and ISIS representatives, ISIS fighters rejected multiple attempts to negotiate an exit corridor for civilians.[13]

ISIS was also adept at using information operations to sway popular support away from coalition and partner forces. Some of the group's influence operations aimed to diminish the legitimacy of the SDF fighting to retake Raqqa. For example, a 2017 analysis of the campaign asserts that ISIS's "monopoly over propaganda in its areas might have altered people's attitudes towards [Kurdish forces]."[14] As evidenced in Mosul and other areas previously under its control, ISIS consistently and adeptly exploited local political fault lines to launch violent attacks and cast itself as the defender of local populations—especially Sunni Arabs. In Raqqa, ISIS was often quick to use social media and other messaging platforms in the wake of successful attacks against the SDF to highlight the inability of U.S. forces to protect local populations. A small-unit commander active in Syria explained, "A classic tactic was motorcycles attacking SDF checkpoints. Then [ISIS] would launch an immediate messaging campaign centered on the fact that U.S.-backed security forces were unable to protect the roads."[15] Because ISIS maintained strict control over the information environment, local reporting was complicated and curtailed, which rendered open-source intelligence (OSINT) collection extremely difficult.[16]

Months before the operation to recapture the city began in June 2017, ISIS fighters who were from Raqqa melted back into the local population. Most of ISIS's senior leadership had also withdrawn from Raqqa to eastern Syria, so by September 2017, all high-value ISIS targets had either left or were already dead.[17] At that point, the city was defended by a dedicated coterie of fighters willing to inflict as much harm as possible on their enemy and on Raqqa civilians.[18] The presence of these foreign fighters ultimately complicated efforts to broker ceasefires and increased the level of violence against civilians.[19]

In sum, ISIS's tactics all significantly increased the probability that civilians would be harmed during the operation to retake the city. Coalition air and ground forces, as well as the SDF, faced enormous challenges identifying the locations of civilians and separating them from combatants.

---

[13] Kurdish civilian activist who was a direct observer in the battle, interview with the authors, July 1, 2020.

[14] Hassan Hassan, "The Battle for Raqqa and the Challenges After Liberation," *CTC Sentinel,* Vol. 10, No. 6, June/July 2017.

[15] U.S. military tactical ground unit operator, interview with the authors, May 2020.

[16] *OSINT* is intelligence that is produced from publicly available information and collected, exploited, and disseminated in a timely manner to an appropriate audience for the purpose of addressing a specific intelligence requirement (U.S. Code, Title 50, Section 3038, Responsibilities of Secretary of Defense Pertaining to National Intelligence Program, 2014).

[17] Hassan, 2017.

[18] Hassan, 2017.

[19] Hassan, 2017.

CHAPTER SIX

Civilian-Harm Mitigation Challenges for Air Forces

Airpower played a significant role in the liberation of Raqqa, during which coalition air operators released some of the highest totals of munitions of the entire air campaign against ISIS. According to U.S. Air Forces Central, in August 2017 alone, U.S. and coalition aircraft released 5,075 munitions, which at the time was the largest single-month total of OIR.[1] Although coalition partners, including the United Kingdom and France, conducted some air strikes, the Raqqa offensive was predominantly a U.S. operation.[2] MQ-1 Predators and MQ-9 Reapers, which provided close air support, tactical reconnaissance, and overwatch of the SDF, conducted approximately 20 percent of coalition strikes in Raqqa.[3] A-10 ground attack aircraft delivered close air support 20 hours a day during the Raqqa offensive and dropped about 44 percent of the weapons around Raqqa for the first two and a half months of the battle.[4] The A-10's capacity to carry a combination of munitions and provide close air support capability made it an attractive option for the SOF community coordinating strikes in Raqqa.[5] Other coalition members also contributed to air strikes in Raqqa: U.K. Typhoons, Tornados, and Reapers contributed to close air support for the SDF and to armed reconnaissance missions and dynamic strikes on ISIS targets.[6]

Although air operators reported receiving clear guidance on civilian casualty mitigation, the application of this guidance was challenging in practice because of limited battlefield-shaping during the seizure of Raqqa, leading to an extremely high proportion of dynamic strikes among all strikes. Despite these challenges, which stemmed from both intentional strategic choices and a complex operating environment, air operators employed several tactics to mitigate civilian harm during operations.

---

1 U.S. Air Forces Central, Combined Air Operations Center, "Airpower Summary," October 31, 2017.

2 Jennifer Hlad, "Punching Above Their Weight," *Air Force Magazine*, November 21, 2017; and Adam J. Hebert, "In Case You Missed It: Airpower Killed ISIS," *Air Force Magazine*, January 29, 2018.

3 Christian Clausen, "Combat RPAs Integral in Defeating ISIS," 432nd Wing/432nd Air Expeditionary Wing Public Affairs, December 5, 2017.

4 Amy McCullough and Brian W. Everstine, "Moody's Flying Tigers Wrap-Up Intense Deployment Fighting ISIS," *Air Force Magazine*, January 10, 2018; and Hlad, 2017. One report described the A-10 as the "workhorse" of the anti-ISIS Coalition (Chad Garland, "A-10 Warthog Drops 2,000-Pound Bunker-Buster on ISIS Sniper Nest in Raqqa," *Stars and Stripes*, August 31, 2017).

5 John Matsumura, John Gordon IV, and Randall Steeb, *Defining an Approach for Future Close Air Support Capability*, Santa Monica, Calif.: RAND Corporation, RR-1233-A, 2017.

6 U.K. Ministry of Defence, "RAF Air Strikes in Iraq and Syria: June 2017," September 5, 2018b.

Deliberate Targeting to Shape the Battlefield Was Insufficient During the Battle for Raqqa

One of the primary obstacles that air—and ground—forces faced when working to minimize civilian harm was the insufficient shaping of the battlefield during every phase of the Raqqa operation.[7] Deliberate targeting operations, a fundamental component of U.S. Air Force and joint doctrine, help to shape the battlefield by striking enemy targets ahead of the ground maneuver.[8] These efforts (which could be called the *deep fight*) reduce the resistance that the ground forces face by eliminating enemy fighters, as well as their command and control, lines of communication and logistics, and ability to build defensive positions. Close air support (which could be called the *close fight*), though an important mission when ground forces are in contact with enemy forces, is generally seen by airpower theorists as an inefficient use of airpower in the aggregate because its effects are essentially tactical.[9] As then–Lt Gen Charles Q. Brown, the Combined Forces Air Component commander during OIR, explained, "I know where the next fight is going to be, [so] what I want to be able to do is actually soften that up with strikes ahead of the ground maneuver. . . . My goal is to . . . strike [ISIS] fighters in advance, as opposed to striking them when they're in contact."[10]

However, we found little evidence of kinetic shaping in Raqqa, as well as limited deliberate targeting beyond the leading edge of the fight during the seizure of the city. According to one general officer, "the net effect of this approach was that all strikes were dynamic, and it took more dynamic strikes to get through the city."[11] By the end of the campaign, as the SDF cleared Raqqa block by block, almost all air strikes were dynamic.[12] Dynamic air strikes launched in urban areas in self-defense of ground forces inherently carry greater risk of civilian casualties because of the compressed timeline in which they occur, which in turn limits the situational awareness of coalition forces. Moreover, targets nominated in self-defense situations do not need to go through the same sequences of approvals and checks, including a full CDE.

Interviewees identified several root causes for the limited shaping operations during the seizure of Raqqa. The primary limitation of shaping during seizure was the lack of a coalition operational-level headquarters for the Raqqa operation to lead deliberate targeting efforts and the lack of targeting teams resourced to conduct the intelligence fusion needed for targeting. The policy decision to give SOJTF-OIR control of the counter-ISIS campaign in Syria meant that SOF directed the airspace.[13] The SOF community's traditional strengths, such as striking terrorist targets and working with irregular partners, were vital to the operation, but SOF leaders and operators had less experience coordinating a more conventional battle like the one in Raqqa. Without a staff and fusion cells to run deliberate targeting operations, SOJTF-OIR

[7] U.S. military general officer, interview with the authors, May 2020.

[8] Air Force Annex 3-60, 2019.

[9] Phillip S. Meilinger, "Air Strategy Targeting for Effect," *Aerospace Power Journal*, Winter 1999.

[10] Charles Q. Brown, Jr., and Jeff Davis, "Department of Defense Press Briefing by Lt. Gen. Brown via Teleconference from Southwest Asia," transcript, U.S. Department of Defense, May 27, 2016.

[11] U.S. military general officer, interview with the authors, May 2020.

[12] U.S. air unit operator, interview with the authors, April 2020.

[13] SOJTF-OIR was the coalition's lead in advising and supporting liberating Raqqa from November 2016–2017 (Raqqa Study Group, 2018, p. 3).

focused on providing close air support to the SDF rather than on shaping the battlespace with deliberate strikes.[14] According to one general officer, this "thin approach to warfighting got the job done but with a lot of shortcuts, and the ability to target beyond the leading edge of the fight was sacrificed."[15]

Compounding the lack of an operational headquarters to run shaping operations was a slow and protracted deliberate targeting process at the Combined Air Operations Center in Qatar. According to one CJTF-OIR official, deliberate targets took an average of 35 days to germinate from target discovery to full approval by the Joint Targeting Coordination Board during the start of the battle for Raqqa; this gave ISIS the ability to move locations and preserve its capabilities without the risk of being struck.[16] Additionally, the prioritization of scarce ISR assets to provide close air support missions limited the development of deliberate targets. Former CJTF-OIR Commander Sean MacFarland reflected on the difficulty of taking ISR assets away from the close fight to support the deep fight: "I had to divert resources from [the close] fight in order to go after these [deep-fight] targets . . . . And of course, . . . any time you try to move a UAV [unmanned aerial vehicle] line someplace, there's wailing and gnashing of teeth."[17] MacFarland later explained that the coalition was disinclined to pull "ISR away for targets that weren't well developed," especially when he "couldn't point to a bad guy like in the close fight."[18] Nevertheless, one CJTF-OIR official noted that, without an operational-level headquarters and well-resourced targeting teams to direct ISR to support shaping operations, "even if all the ISR in the world had gone to Raqqa, it would have not resulted in more shaping once seizure [of the city] started."[19]

In sum, the insufficiency of shaping operations during the isolation and seizure phases of the battle for Raqqa was one of the most-important factors that led to the high proportion of dynamic strikes during the operation; it also reveals the importance of operational design in future urban operations. Conducting sufficient shaping operations would have allowed coalition forces to "design [their] maneuver around [the] human terrain [in the city]."[20] As one military official explained, "If you're serious about reducing CIVCAS [civilian casualties], you can design the operation around where your humans are."[21] Instead, in Raqqa, the coalition was "forced to fight the battle the enemy want[ed]."[22]

---

[14] U.S. military general officer, interview with the authors, May 2020.

[15] U.S. military general officer, interview with the authors, September 2020.

[16] U.S. military general officer, interview with the authors, September 2020. The deliberate targeting process begins with the CJTF-OIR commander periodically issuing guidance for the campaign through the Joint Targeting Coordination Board, a group formed by the commander to accomplish broad targeting oversight functions that may include but are not limited to coordinating targeting information; providing targeting guidance, synchronization, and priorities; and refining the joint integrated prioritized target list. See Joint Publication 3-60, 2018.

[17] Foundation for Defense of Democracies and the Brookings Institution, "Economic Defeat of the Islamic State: Behind the Scenes of Operation Tidal Wave II," panel, May 10, 2019.

[18] Becca Wasser, Stacie L. Pettyjohn, Jeffrey Martini, Alexandra T. Evans, Karl P. Mueller, Nathaniel Edenfield, Gabrielle Tarini, Ryan Haberman, and Jalen Zeman, *The Air War Against the Islamic State: The Role of Airpower in Operation Inherent Resolve*, Santa Monica, Calif.: RAND Corporation, RR-A388-1, 2021, p. 223.

[19] U.S. military general officer, interview with the authors, September 2020.

[20] U.S. military general officer, interview with the authors, May 2020.

[21] U.S. military general officer, interview with the authors, May 2020.

[22] U.S. military general officer, interview with the authors, May 2020.

The Complexity of Raqqa's Urban Environment Increased Civilian Casualties and Infrastructure Damage

The complexity of the urban environment in and around Raqqa also compounded the challenges that air planners and operators faced in minimizing harm to civilians. As one operator put it, "How do you shoot a weapon down an alley while you're flying a plane?"[23] Many neighborhoods in Raqqa consisted of concrete, mid-rise apartment blocks. The layout and architecture of the city meant that it was difficult to know with a high degree of certainty that a strike would not lead to civilian casualties. As a result, air operators "had to get creative to figure out ways to strike targets at the bottom of" the city's apartment buildings.[24] They were "constantly balancing where the good guys and the civilians" were located and asking, "Is that building the building I need [to drop]?"[25] One air operator described the urban warfare that characterized the Raqqa offensive as "a different problem set" that U.S. pilots "had not trained for prior to showing up" in theater.[26] Although the coalition was able to draw some lessons from previous engagements in the Middle East, such as Operation Iraqi Freedom, the size, scale, and scope of the Raqqa campaign presented new challenges. It was a "very, very challenging tactical and operational problem" from the perspective of air operators.[27]

Air Operators Took Important Tactical Steps to Mitigate Civilian Harm

Over the past two decades, the U.S. Air Force has developed tools, tactics, technologies, and concepts to mitigate civilian harm, in line with its institutional and operational emphasis on greater precision, less destruction, and economy of force.[28] We found that, for the most part, during the liberation of Raqqa, air operators implemented many of the civilian casualty mitigation techniques and lessons that the Air Force has learned during previous operations.[29]

For example, the use of precision-guided munitions played a significant role in reducing civilian harm in Raqqa.[30] During the offensive, precision-guided munitions "provide[d] commanders with precise, deliberate, proportionate effects," allowing them to "tak[e] all feasible measures to protect civilians from harm."[31] Pilots employed a variety of munitions to tailor strikes to reduce collateral damage in the city, including low-yield weapons, such as the GBU-39 Small Diameter Bomb, and low-fragmentation weapons, such as the GBU-54(V).[32] The use of Reaper

---

23 U.S. air unit operator, interview with the authors, April 2020.

24 Hebert, 2018.

25 U.S. air unit operator, interview with the authors, May 2020.

26 U.S. air unit operator, interview with the authors, April 2020.

27 U.S. air unit operator, interview with the authors, April 2020.

28 Sewall, 2016, pp. 147–167.

29 Many of these institutional adaptions and techniques are documented in Sewall, 2016, pp. 147–167.

30 U.S. Air Force general officer, interview with the authors, May 2020. According to the general officer, the employment of laser-guided rockets in particular represents one of the most-important recent contributions of weaponeering to the reduction of civilian harm.

31 Matthew Isler, "Department of Defense Press Briefing by Brig. Gen. Matthew Isler on Central Command's Targeting and Civilian Casualty Investigation Processes," transcript, U.S. Department of Defense October 25, 2017.

32 Wasser et al, 2021, p. 192.

drones, which were armed with laser-guided precision weapons and "figured prominently" into the Raqqa offensive, also facilitated the reduction of civilian casualties in the city.[33] Precision munitions, including Joint Direct Attack Munitions, were a "very closely managed commodity during the Raqqa offensive. The extensive use of these weapons in Operation Inherent Resolve at times led to shortages, resulting in the Air Force drawing on stocks from other theaters."[34]

During the first weeks of the Raqqa offensive, pilots often found that they were not carrying the weapons they needed for a particular strike. This issue arose partly because air tasking orders required a certain amount of time within a 72-hour planning cycle to adequately prepare the weapons and load the aircraft and partly because operators needed to learn ISIS's tactics and the terrain in the Raqqa battlespace. According to one air operator who flew in Raqqa, "at the beginning, certain weapons were called for, but you weren't carrying them. In this case, you would usually err on the side of being more cautious to try to come as close to the effect as you could without going overboard."[35] The Air Force quickly adapted and started loading fighters "buffet style," or with a variety of weapons that might be needed.[36] Air operators reported that about two to three weeks after the start of the operation, they regularly loaded fighter jets with the right mix of precision-guided munitions.[37] According to an official with experience on the OIR joint targeting board, although there were likely instances when jets were not loaded with the ideal munitions, the 72-hour window is a "best-case" timeline and was not rigid, because the desired effect from the commander or the details about the target may change; other OIR officials reported being able to change weapon configurations well inside of the 72-hour window.[38] One OIR official noted that the two-week delay that Air Force operators reported in Raqqa before planes began carrying the ideal mix of munitions could have been because of the need to quickly adjust after confronting ISIS fighters, their equipment, and the material of structures in real time.[39]

Nevertheless, for much of the Raqqa operation, according to the assistant deputy commander of U.S. Air Forces Central, air operators "typically had 10 or more weapons options available . . . in addition to individual fusing options for each of those weapons."[40] This enabled air operators to try lower-yield weapons before employing the higher-yield weapons that might lead to more collateral damage. Finally, air operators used weaponeering techniques to mitigate risks to civilians and infrastructure. For example, pilots tried to minimize the time in flight of a weapon so that ISIS fighters would not have the chance to walk into a crowded area where civilians were present.[41] Air operators also selected delayed fusing for weapons, sometimes up to 45–60 milliseconds to minimize the amount of fragmentation of the bomb.[42]

---

[33] Jeff Daniels, "ISIS Fight Shows US Military Can Use Lower-Cost Weapons with Lethal Results," CNBC, July 19, 2017.

[34] U.S. air unit operator, interview with the authors, April 2020; U.S. general officer, interview with the authors, November 2020.

[35] U.S. air unit operator, interview with the authors, April 2020.

[36] U.S. air unit operator, interview with the authors, April 2020.

[37] U.S. air unit operator, interview with the authors, April 2020.

[38] OIR official, interview with the authors, November 2020; general officer, interview with the authors, September 2020.

[39] OIR official, interview with the authors, November 2020.

[40] Isler, 2017.

[41] U.S. air unit operator, interview with the authors, April 2020.

[42] U.S. air unit operator, interview with the authors, May 2020.

CHAPTER SEVEN

Civilian-Harm Mitigation Challenges for Ground Forces

Ground forces play a critically important role in warfare for several reasons. First, ground forces, particularly infantry forces, interact with local populations to gather information and intelligence that is often critical to achieving tactical and strategic objectives. Second, their presence creates a direct link between the battlefield and supporting elements, such as air assets and artillery units, which can enhance the precision of strikes and minimize harm to surrounding civilians. Third, ground operators provide a readily available capability to conduct targeted raids, obviating the need to drop ordnance from the sky and risk causing harm to civilians. Fourth, if civilians are harmed in the course of operations, ground forces can collect information from local populations to inform civilian casualty assessments and ultimately initiate the process of civilian casualty response. Of course, an obvious risk to relying on ground forces is the potential for casualties. In response, recent U.S. military operations have shifted away from a heavy reliance on infantry forces and toward force structures that primarily employ airpower and artillery, among other elements, to increase survivability on the battlefield. But this move has come at a cost; these types of force structures inhibit the level of information collection and vetting that ground forces would otherwise accomplish through their interactions with locals, and the structures lack the other aforementioned capabilities that ground forces contribute to the fight. Their structural design leaves them largely starved of local information, less knowledgeable about the civilian environment, and less able to discern noncombatants from combatants. Ultimately, force structures that rely less on infantry forces are more at risk of causing civilian harm, if inadvertently.

These dynamics were at play during the battle to retake Raqqa from ISIS, which was first and foremost a partner-led operation that relied little on U.S. ground forces, especially infantry forces. SDF fighters served as the lead maneuver element in the campaign, with substantial support from U.S. and coalition air and artillery assets. This structure presented specific challenges to U.S. ground forces, and that experience provides valuable lessons for mitigating and responding to civilian harm in the context of close-quarters urban warfare. In this chapter, we highlight several challenges that the Raqqa campaign posed for U.S. ground forces. First, the very nature of urban combat made precision targeting particularly difficult for ground forces, especially artillery units situated just outside Raqqa. Two additional challenges around mitigating civilian harm stemmed from dynamics internal to coalition ground forces that participated in the Raqqa campaign. Specifically, our research showed that units involved in the campaign were, at times, inadequately prepared for operating as a joint force or faced challenges insofar as different services adhered to different operational cultures on how best to mitigate civilian harm. Moreover, the frequent rotation of ground forces assigned to support the Raqqa campaign—particularly conventional forces—caused some messaging and best practices around mitigating civilian harm to become lost as units moved in and out of the area.

Finally, in this chapter, we briefly highlight the notion that partnered operations, by definition, limit the extent to which U.S. forces can take the lead in operations. This dynamic was relevant in Raqqa and sometimes had the effect of curtailing the amount of control that U.S. ground forces had over efforts to mitigate civilian harm. Chapter Eight provides a fuller discussion of the United States' partner force, the SDF.

A Densely Packed Urban Environment Posed Challenges for Artillery Units

U.S. ground forces supporting the SDF in the campaign to reclaim Raqqa from ISIS control consisted of SOF, including U.S. Army Rangers, and conventional forces, specifically USMC infantry and artillery units from the 11th and 24th Marine Expeditionary Units.[1] U.S. and coalition forces used a wide array of munitions during the campaign; U.S. conventional ground units in particular relied on M777A2 Howitzers, which mostly launched 155-mm shells equipped with the XM1156 Precision Guidance Kit, and employed High Mobility Artillery Rocket Systems with 227-mm rockets directed by the Global Positioning System.[2]

The urban battlefield posed especially significant challenges for U.S. artillery units charged with providing support to SDF fighters operating within the city limits. Indeed, NGO officials expressed deep concerns about the continued use of artillery in Raqqa, whether precision-guided or not.[3] Nevertheless, precision-guided artillery provided what some military operators considered one of the best weaponeering solutions in Raqqa, given that the use of such munitions requires adherence to five requirements for accurate fire.[4] Had artillery units not adhered to these requirements, any precision rounds launched into the city would have amounted to expensive "dumb rounds."[5] When all five requirements are consistently met, precision-guidance kits and Excalibur rounds offer a circular error probable (i.e., a measure of precision) that is far below that advertised in the weapons' published performance parameters.[6]

By March 2017, elements from the 11th Marine Expeditionary Unit had set up an artillery battery of Howitzers and other cannons in the vicinity of Raqqa, approximately 20 km

---

[1] An artillery battery from the 11th Marine Expeditionary Unit went ashore to provide artillery support to Kurdish and Syrian Arab forces expected to launch an offensive against Raqqa in early 2017. The unit was replaced by an artillery battery from the 24th Marine Expeditionary Unit around May 2017.

[2] Thomas Gibbons-Neff, "Marine Unit in Syria Using Highly Advanced Artillery Ammunition, Video Shows," *Washington Post,* July 3, 2017; Mackenzie Wolf, "Marine Corps Artillery Support Vital as the Fight for Raqqa Intensifies," *Military Times*, June 27, 2017; and Lamothe and Gibbons-Neff, 2017.

[3] Amnesty International, 2018; NGO official, interview with the authors, March 2020.

[4] To achieve accurate first-round fire for effect on a target, artillery units must meet five requirements related to target location and size; firing unit location; weapon and ammunition information; meteorological information; and computational procedures. If each of these requirements is met, the firing unit will be able to deliver accurate and timely fires in support of ground maneuver elements. See Field Manual 6-40, *Tactics, Techniques, and Procedures for the Field Artillery Manual Cannon Gunnery,* Washington, D.C.: U.S. Marine Corps, October 1999.

[5] U.S. Army artillery officer, correspondence with the authors, November 2020.

[6] U.S. Army artillery officer, correspondence with the authors, November 2020.

outside the city limits.[7] The guns were deliberately positioned within range of the front lines inside Raqqa to respond to rapidly changing situations. The artillery Marines' principal mission was to disrupt ISIS lines of communications and provide suppressive fires in support of SDF fighters moving into Raqqa during the battle's initial phases and then maneuvering in the city during later phases. Marines positioned outside Raqqa fired a large number of the aforementioned 155-mm rounds fitted with the XM1156 Precision Guidance Kit, which is less accurate than other precision kits (such as the XM982 Excalibur) but simpler to use and a less expensive munition.[8] The responsiveness and relative precision of these artillery units, relative to some other fires employed during the campaign, were especially valuable when it came to suppressing ISIS fighters inside the city; artillery units could rapidly adjust fires to disrupt militants as they fell back and took up new positions in the city. In some cases, rapidly adjustable artillery fire likely helped mitigate some civilian harm when ISIS and SDF fighters were extremely close together in areas where civilians were also present.

Some military operators with experience in Iraq speculated that many of the artillery rounds fired during the campaign to retake Raqqa were M825 white phosphorous rounds used to create smoke screens and illumination rounds that provided visibility for forces operating at night.[9] Our research, however, indicated that, although this may have been the case in Mosul and some other places, very few of these rounds were used in Raqqa. In fact, Secretary of Defense Mattis issued an order following operations in Mosul disallowing the use of white phosphorous munitions because of their incendiary effects.[10] It is important to understand the differences between illumination rounds and white phosphorous (smoke) rounds. Illumination rounds do not pose significant risk to civilians, relative to high-explosive incendiary ammunition; the spent canister is the only material that comes down after the round is fired, and the likelihood of it striking a civilian or structure with enough force to cause damage is minimal.[11] White phosphorous rounds, on the other hand, pose more risks to civilians and surrounding structures, given the extremely high temperatures at which the munitions burn and the toxicity of the fumes.[12] Nevertheless, smoke rounds have proven valuable in efforts to protect civilians from harm in contexts similar to Raqqa. In Mosul, for example, U.S. Army artillery units successfully created smokescreens to enable Iraqi forces to rescue dozens of civilians being held hostage by enemy forces and help them escape from ISIS-controlled areas.[13]

In short, the main advantage of artillery batteries situated in close proximity to Raqqa was that they provided a readily available, all-weather fire support asset; rapidly adjustable fire was especially valuable in a context as fluid as Raqqa.[14] Nevertheless, urban environments create many challenges to achieving both good situational awareness and accurate fires. Near

---

[7] Gibbons-Neff, 2017.

[8] Joseph Trevithick, "Marines 'Burned Out' Two Howitzer Barrels During the Raqqa Offensive," *The Drive*, November 3, 2017.

[9] U.S. military tactical ground unit operators, interview with the authors, June 2020.

[10] DoD official, interview with the authors, March 2020.

[11] George Will, "Avoiding Collateral Damage," *Press Telegram*, September 1, 2017.

[12] Daniel C. Gibson, Scott Pence, and Stoney Grimes, "Smoke Employment in the Battle for Mosul," *Field Artillery Professional Bulletin*, No. 3, 2020.

[13] Gibson, Pence, and Grimes, 2020.

[14] Gibson, Pence, and Grimes, 2020; Trevithick, 2017.

misses of just several meters can lead to civilian casualties in a densely populated neighborhood, so artillery forces must be deliberate and disciplined in achieving the five requirements for accurate fires. One way to address this challenge is by scaling up training in urban combat operations so that it is based on scenarios involving (1) enemy and U.S. forces in close proximity in an urban environment and (2) civilian casualty incidents similar to those incurred during the battle for Raqqa. Such training could further familiarize operators with precision-guidance technologies available for artillery, improve the precision with which artillery units launch high numbers of strikes at rapid rates, and provide opportunities to further improve discipline around the five requirements for accurate fires.

Ground Forces Struggled to Operate as Part of a Joint Force and Overcome Coordination Seams

U.S. ground forces participating in the campaign to liberate Raqqa also faced challenges in surmounting the coordination seams that come with operating as part of a joint force. For the most part, U.S. conventional ground forces and their SOF counterparts operated without significant conflict or controversy. According to subject-matter experts, this was particularly true in the case of operations conducted jointly between Marines and SOF operators.[15] SOF ground forces were especially eager to operate with self-sustaining forces, making Marine units well-suited to supporting SOF, because of their expeditionary mission. However, our interviews with U.S. military ground force operators also suggest that tensions did arise at times between the various services, including around the issue of civilian harm. Disconnects typically arose for one of two reasons.

First, some operators highlighted the sometimes divergent attitudes around civilian harm that existed across the services: "Because of philosophical differences between SOF and the regular Army, there was a communications gap. Marines also had a different perspective. Everyone is part of the joint force, but people had different attitudes about the mission."[16] Differences in debrief cultures across the various services may have also made a difference in how operators drew on and internalized lessons learned over the course of the campaign. Although some services are more likely to consistently debrief their forces after specific operations, others do so less systematically and tend to conduct debriefs only when something goes wrong.[17] In other words, although DoD may issue clear guidance around the topic of civilian harm, the various ways that different services train their forces to specific standards, disseminate messaging around mitigating and responding to civilian casualties, and develop debrief cultures around the issue may create fissures within the joint force during active operations.

Moreover, U.S. military operators largely agree that the effective communication of intent around specific issues, including civilian harm, hinges on the existence of personal relationships.[18] One operator explained his experiences as follows: "If SOF sees the issue the same way as OIR sees the issue, it is going to mitigate a lot of problems around civilian casualties.

[15] RAND subject-matter expert, interview with the authors, February 2020.

[16] Former U.S. military tactical ground unit commander, interview with the authors, April 2020.

[17] U.S. air unit commander, interview with the authors, May 2020.

[18] U.S. military tactical ground unit operator, interview with the authors, May 2020.

If gaps are not bridged, there are going to be problems."[19] But effectively disseminating commander's intent on various issues is harder in joint environments, a challenge that remains relatively unaddressed in pre-deployment training and once troops arrive in theater. During planning meetings in the lead-up to the battle for Raqqa, for example, some operators recalled seeing different perspectives emerge as various elements sought to assert their authority over specific missions.[20]

Second, and relatedly, messaging and experience around mitigating and responding to civilian harm was often lost as various units and forces rotated in and out of the area during the Raqqa campaign. USMC and Army units tapped to support SOF operations, for example, remained in-country for six to seven months, during which they built significant experience dealing with civilian-harm issues. When these forces rotated out and were replaced by new units, the learning process essentially had to begin anew. As noted by a U.S. ground forces commander, "At the start of every tour, there will be a dip in proficiency and attention to the civilian casualty issues on the part of rotating units. It takes about 30 to 60 days for proficiency to rise; the level of [battlefield] intensity influences the learning curve around the issue too."[21] Although conventional ground forces strive to overcome these challenges, they face several barriers, including weak or nonexistent information technology connections between deployed and deploying units, intervening echelons of command, and decisions to rotate commands despite the proven benefits of continuity. SOF were somewhat more immune to these challenges, given their shorter but more-frequent tours in-country and the extent to which SOF operators stayed connected to the theater during dwell time through a more robust network. The U.S. ground forces commander noted, "[SOF] operators were never 'off' and never completely disengaged" from the battlefield.[22]

In sum, these challenges highlight the importance of adjusting pre-deployment exercises to integrate more opportunities for consistent and joint training around the issue of civilian harm, as well as offering continuous training on the issue while units are deployed in theater. Pre-deployment training not only can improve by exposing fighting units to the complexities of mitigating and responding to civilian harm before they reach theater but also can expose disparate units and services to the complexities inherent in working as part of a diverse, joint force in high-risk environments. Additional opportunities for joint training can also further highlight the importance of maintaining coherent and unified messaging around civilian harm, creating an aperture for ground operators and other units to understand the coalition or joint perspective on the topic.[23] In other words, civilian harm is as much an institutional issue—including how the U.S. military mans, trains, and equips the force—as it is an operational issue. As one commander of U.S. ground forces put it, "the best practices [in mitigating and responding to civilian harm] remain what they have always been: thorough training, rehearsal, the use of vignettes, debriefs, after-action reports from theater, etc. Then feeding all of this back to the U.S. to units preparing for deployment."[24] Other commanders also

[19] Former U.S. military tactical ground unit commander, interview with the authors, April 2020.

[20] Former U.S. military tactical ground unit commander, interview with the authors, April 2020.

[21] U.S. ground forces commander, interview with the authors, April 2020.

[22] U.S. ground forces commander, interview with the authors, April 2020.

[23] U.S. air unit commander, interview with the authors, May 2020.

[24] U.S. ground forces commander, interview with the authors, May 2020.

noted that the simulation enterprise should more widely integrate civilian casualty scenarios into its products.[25]

The aforementioned challenges also underscore the critical role that clearly communicated commander's intent around civilian harm plays in ensuring that all services and units contributing to a joint operation view the issue through the same lens. One U.S. ground force commander commented that, although commander's intent may be particularly difficult to disseminate in joint environments, "making sure the whole force is approaching a topic area on the same sheet of music is critical."[26]

Partnered Operations Created Policymaking Dilemmas

U.S. policy decisions around the counter-ISIS campaign placed significant restrictions on the actions of U.S. ground forces during the battle for Raqqa. Authorities governing the role of U.S. forces in Syria and Iraq changed over the course of 2016 and slowly allowed U.S. ground forces to provide closer advise-assist-accompany support to partners, such as the SDF. For example, DoD lifted certain policy restrictions that had otherwise forced U.S. troops to maintain their positions at the last point of cover and concealment in late 2016 and early 2017, effectively bringing ground forces closer to dynamic action alongside partner forces. The decision may have helped partner forces better mitigate the potential for civilian harm, but one could also argue that bringing U.S. ground forces closer to the action increased those forces' responsibility for civilian casualty events.[27] These dynamics bring to the fore the delicate balance that U.S. policymakers and military operators must strike when dealing with civilian-harm issues in the context of partnered operations. In the next chapter, we discuss the U.S. partner force in Raqqa, the SDF, in more detail and further explore the dilemmas of partnered operations there.

---

[25] U.S. air unit commanders, interview with the authors, May 2020.

[26] Former U.S. military tactical unit commander, interview with the authors, April 2020.

[27] DoD Office of the General Counsel personnel, interview with the authors, March 2020.

CHAPTER EIGHT

Civilian-Harm Mitigation Challenges Working by, with, and Through Partners

When fighting with or relying on partner military forces, the U.S. military does not fully control the actions of key actors with whom it is associated on the ground. In some cases, local partner forces may have some advantages over U.S. forces in terms of mitigating civilian harm. For example, because of their language and cultural fluency, local forces might be able to better distinguish between combatants and civilians or better discern hostile intent from behavior that is locally normative.[1] For example, in Raqqa and in the resulting operations down the Euphrates River Valley, the participation of Arab partners in the SDF was critical to leading discussions with local tribal leaders to protect civilians.[2] Involving a local force in military operations can also be a meaningful way to empower local residents to report civilian harm.

In other instances, however, working with partners—whose interests, priorities, and capabilities may not necessarily align with those of the United States—can complicate the U.S. military's ability to mitigate civilian harm. For example, in terms of priorities and capabilities, partner forces' military doctrines may or may not include guidance or codes of conduct for mitigating and responding to civilian harm. Partners may not have command cultures in which civilian protection practices are institutionalized or enforced. Certain partner forces may lack robust capabilities, such as ISR or CDE software, that help prevent and assess civilian harm. Partner forces may be insufficiently trained on practices for mitigating civilian harm and might understand just the basic requirements of the law of war. Some partner forces may also simply have a higher tolerance for civilian harm and be willing to take greater risk, relative to the United States. Furthermore, relying on partner forces might leave U.S. forces vulnerable to faulty intelligence or manipulation that could increase harm to civilians. A dependence on partner forces to accomplish military objectives in situations in which U.S. forces have a limited military footprint may also constrain the ability of the United States to apply pressure or impose conditions on partners to reduce civilian harm for fear of losing that partner's cooperation. Finally, when working with local partners, there may not be a legitimate U.S.-recognized, central government to take responsibility for balancing the risks to civilians against the need to achieve mission goals.

Despite the risks and limitations of relying on partner militaries, U.S. policymakers chose to rely on a local partner in Syria, the SDF. It is difficult, and perhaps impossible, to isolate precisely how the SDF might have contributed to civilian harm or civilian protection, given

[1] Larry Lewis and Sarah Holewinski, "Changing of the Guard: Civilian Protection for an Evolving Military," *Prism*, Vol. 4, No. 2, 2013, p. 62.

[2] Retired senior military officer, interview with the authors, July 2020.

the multitude of players in Raqqa and the surrounding areas in eastern Syria. Nevertheless, in this chapter, we provide several observations on the ways in which the unique nature of the SDF might have mitigated, or contributed to, civilian harm in Raqqa. We begin by providing some background and context on the SDF's origins and how the United States chose to train and equip its partner force.

The Origins, Composition, and Geopolitical Dilemmas of the SDF

The SDF played the main ground combat role in military operations against ISIS in Raqqa. Established in late 2015 as a result of ad-hoc cooperation with U.S. forces against ISIS, the SDF was an umbrella group initially led by and composed of YPG fighters. The U.S. partnership with a primarily Kurdish force angered the Turkish government, which considered the YPG and its political parent organization (the Democratic Union Party) to be the Syrian arm of the Kurdistan Workers Party, a terrorist organization.[3] As the fight against ISIS progressed, the United States attempted to placate Turkish concerns by recruiting additional Arab fighters to the SDF's ranks.[4] Nevertheless, Turkish pressure meant that the group received only limited military equipment—less than would be considered necessary for the SDF to successfully accomplish its mission without substantial U.S. support.[5] In addition, prior to the Raqqa operation, U.S. military equipment was supplied to only the Arab factions inside the SDF, the Syrian Arab Coalition.

The transformation of the SDF to incorporate additional Arab forces was also important to help the group capture and control predominantly Arab territory controlled by ISIS in Syria, including Raqqa, with forces that were local to the places being captured. In theory, a majority-Arab force could help protect civilians by employing fighters who shared the same ethnicity as civilians and who were possibly from the territories being liberated. This was difficult to implement in practice, however, because the SDF's leadership remained Kurdish, and the Kurdish units were the ones with the experience, training, and relationships with U.S. forces.[6] Even though the SDF is a decentralized organization, the Syrian Arabs who were recruited into the SDF were often deployed to hold, stabilize, and police territory, and Kurdish YPG units commanded troops on the front lines. This arrangement largely resulted from the experience in Manbij, Syria, in 2016, where U.S. forces encouraged the YPG to allow Arab forces to take the lead, but that resulted in significant SDF causalities and emphasized the criticality of the YPG as the fighting backbone of the group.

Moreover, SDF fighters local to Raqqa did not participate substantially in the operation there. According to Kurdish sources, the commander of Liwa Thuwwar Raqqa, a component

---

[3] Both Turkey and the United States have designated the Kurdistan Worker's Party a terrorist organization. However, the United States does not consider the YPG or the Democratic Union Party to be terrorist organizations. See Congressional Research Service, 2017.

[4] From 2015 to the start of the Raqqa operation in 2017, the SDF went from a primarily Kurdish force to a majority Arab force of approximately 50,000 troops ("US Commander Says Syrian Arab Coalition Is Now Majority Group Within SDF," *Rudaw*, March 3, 2017; and senior military officers, interview with the authors, July 2020).

[5] State Department official, interview with the authors, June 2020.

[6] Senior DoD official, interview with the authors, March 3, 2020; State Department counter-ISIS official, interview with the authors, June 4, 2020.

of the SDF from Raqqa city, wanted to separate his forces from the SDF to lead the battle to capture Raqqa and become the city's new governor.[7] This testimony is disputed by Arab sources local to Raqqa, who argue that the commander was simply trying to put his troops on the front line in order to mitigate harm to civilians.[8] The tensions between the SDF's mission and the commander of Liwa Thuwwar Raqqa's desire to lead the liberation of Raqqa meant that the fighters most local to Raqqa were not able to meaningfully participate in the battle to capture the city from ISIS. Several officials, operators, and journalists interviewed for this report noted that, because SDF units on the front lines had few social ties to the local population and lacked knowledge of the human terrain, they might have had a reduced incentive and ability to preserve the city.[9] For example, according to one Arab journalist from Raqqa,

> When these fighters were in the city, they were Kurds. When a[n ISIS] fighter shot at them from a building, they didn't care; they would just open up their iPad and call an air strike on the building. One battalion [that joined the Raqqa operation was] . . . from Tabqa city . . . and you could see the effect they had on the operation [to capture Tabqa, a battle that took place earlier in 2017] because they took care of their city, and you can see that Tabqa was not destroyed.[10]

Training and Equipping the SDF

In 2014, the U.S. Congress authorized and funded a train-and-equip program for vetted Syrian fighters for select purposes, including providing support to forces contributing to the U.S-led effort to defeat ISIS. The program, which originally trained vetted Syrian opposition forces inside Turkey who would then return to Syria to fight ISIS, came under intense scrutiny in summer 2015 after U.S. officials reported that only "four or five" graduates remained in the fight against ISIS, while others had turned over equipment and weaponry to al-Qa'ida affiliates.[11] In October 2015, the Barack Obama administration shifted the approach of the train-and-equip program toward equipping and enabling existing Arab groups under the SDF umbrella. CJTF-OIR received nearly $1.3 billion in military aid and support from 2015 to 2018 under the authority granted by Section 1209 of the fiscal year 2015 National Defense Authorization Act; the allocation was known as the Syria Train and Equip Fund and later the Counter-ISIS Train and Equip Fund.[12]

On May 9, 2017, the Trump administration departed from the previous policy of equipping only Arab elements within the SDF and authorized DoD to "equip Kurdish elements

---

7 Kurdish NGO official, interview with the authors, June 12, 2020.

8 Raqqa journalist, interview with the authors, June 4, 2020.

9 Ground unit operator, interview with the authors, February 2020; NGO official, interview with the authors, March 2020; State Department official, interview with the authors, June 2020.

10 Raqqa journalist, interview with the authors, June 4, 2020.

11 Congressional Research Service, 2017.

12 Raqqah Study Group, 2018, p. 5.

of the SDF as necessary to ensure a clear victory over ISIS in Raqqa."[13] The exact package of weapons transferred from the United States to the YPG is not publicly available, but the Overseas Contingency Operations budget request for the Counter-ISIS Train and Equip Fund in fiscal year 2017 specifies that the lethal equipment requested "may include" small arms (e.g., AK-47s and PKM machine guns), heavy weapons (e.g., DShK machine guns), mortar systems (e.g., 60, 82, and 120 mm), and anti-tank weapons (e.g., SPG-9 guns).[14] According to an OIR spokesperson, as of July 6, 2017, the United States had delivered weapons and ammunition to the SDF, plus more than 400 vehicles and personal equipment for more than 40,000 troops.[15]

The SDF Was a Capable Fighting Force, but Its Norms and Interests on Civilian Protection Were Different from Those of the United States

According to several interviewees, the SDF was a motivated, capable fighting force that shared the United States' goals of defeating ISIS. The interviewees praised SDF fighters as "soldiers the U.S. military could rely on" and "competent planners that understood strategy."[16] Senior military leaders noted that working with the SDF was a "higher level of by, with, and through," meaning that the United States and the SDF had a close relationship and conducted complex urban operations over vast portions of territory.[17] U.S. operators also emphasized the high level of trust between U.S. and SDF personnel, which U.S. forces did not always have with some other partners. For example, SDF leadership did not let unvetted forces near U.S. forces: "They were hypersensitive in this regard, if one of us got hurt, they believed they would lose U.S. backing."[18]

The SDF also understood that civilian casualties were a key driver of U.S. policy and knew that causing high levels of civilian harm would put at risk the United States' ability to support the effort.[19] The SDF also understood the importance of respect for the law of war. One NGO official reflected on the experience providing law of war training to the SDF: "The first impression I got was a sense of professionalism. They knew about the rules. There was clearly an intent and understanding that civilians needed to be protected."[20] The same official

---

[13] Pentagon statement quoted in Michael R. Gordon and Eric Schmitt, "Trump to Arm Syrian Kurds, Even as Turkey Strongly Objects," *New York Times*, May 9, 2017.

[14] Office of the Under Secretary of Defense (Comptroller), *Department of Defense Budget Fiscal Year (FY) 2017: Request for Additional FY 2017 Appropriations—Overseas Contingency Operations (OCO), Counter-Islamic State of Iraq and Syria (ISIS) Train and Equip Fund (CTEF)*, Washington, D.C., March 2017, p. 13.

[15] D. J. Anderson and Jeff Davis, "Department of Defense Press Briefing by Brigadier General Anderson via Teleconference from Iraq," transcript, U.S. Department of Defense, July 6, 2017.

[16] Mick Mulroy, former Deputy Assistant Secretary of Defense for the Middle East and retired CIA paramilitary officer in the Special Activities Center, interview with the authors, March 2020; general officer, interview with the authors, May 2020; State Department official, interview with the authors, June 2020.

[17] Former general officer, interview with the authors, July 2020.

[18] Ground unit operator, interview with the authors, May 2020.

[19] Ground unit operator, interview with the authors, May 2020.

[20] NGO official, interview with the authors, July 2020; this point was reinforced by a former U.S. general officer, interview with the authors, July 2020.

recounted how, during the training in spring 2017, the senior SDF commander left the room to allow his subordinates to speak freely about their mistakes, indicating a desire and willingness to improve.

However, the SDF's norms, risk tolerance, and interests regarding civilian protection were different from those of the United States. For example, according to the same NGO official who provided training to SDF commanders, the SDF might not have classified the families of ISIS fighters as civilians, because of their role in transporting weapons or holding ISIS ideology—a classification that would not be consistent with international law.[21] The United Nations has also documented the SDF's policies of forced conscription, including the conscription of children, and forced internment of noncombatants.[22] Finally, compared with U.S. forces, SDF personnel were generally more tolerant of civilian-harm risk during military operations in Raqqa, giving preference to defeating ISIS and preserving the combat power of their small force. As one senior U.S. official noted, SDF leaders had to manage a tense coalition and economize their force during the Raqqa battle out of fear that some disgruntled elements of the SDF coalition might defect or desert should they suffer high losses.[23] As another U.S. operator noted, "Their end goal is survival. . . . What they are willing to accept in terms of collateral damage is much different than ours. Finding the middle ground in Raqqa was difficult."[24]

U.S. Assistance to the SDF Prioritized Respect for the Law of War but Faced Constraints of Time and Scale

U.S. payments, resupply, and training provided to the SDF were contingent on the partner's compliance with the law of war and respect for human rights. Through the Counter-ISIS Train and Equip Fund, SDF fighters were strictly vetted prior to receiving U.S. training and equipment. However, because coalition assessments of civilian casualties resulting from CJTF-OIR operations did not include instances resulting from SDF operations, U.S. forces did not track or monitor instances of civilian harm caused by the SDF.[25] Most SDF combat units had minimal experience or training in mitigating civilian casualties in high-intensity urban combat environments. Moreover, Turkish pressure on military support for the SDF limited the extent to which those forces could receive basic equipment. "You're asking these guys to take a city with AK-47s," explained a State Department official. Several U.S. military officials noted that, if the SDF had been more heavily armed in Raqqa, it might have reduced the number

---

[21] According to the law of war, those not taking part in hostilities are considered civilians. Thus, ISIS family members would not be considered combatants under the law of war unless they were directly partaking in hostilities (NGO official, interview with the authors, July 2020).

[22] United Nations, *Report of the Independent International Commission of Inquiry on the Syrian Arab Republic*, New York, A/HRC/39/65, August 9, 2018, p. 10.

[23] Former senior State Department official, interview with the authors, July 2020.

[24] U.S. military operator, interview with the authors, April 2020.

[25] Office of the Under Secretary of Defense (Comptroller), 2017, p. 11; Ryan Dillon, "Department of Defense Press Briefing by Col. Dillon via Teleconference from Baghdad, Iraq," transcript, U.S. Department of Defense, June 1, 2017; and Ryan Dillon and Jeff Davis, "Department of Defense Press Briefing by Colonel Dillon via Teleconference from Baghdad, Iraq," transcript, U.S. Department of Defense, June 23, 2017.

of U.S. air strikes needed to support the partner force, which often leveled entire buildings.[26] However, arming a new, relatively inexperienced force more heavily would have presented different civilian-harm mitigation challenges. In terms of training, the need to quickly identify and support a partner force in Syria in the lead-up to the Raqqa offensive, combined with a limited number of U.S. forces in Syria, also meant that the U.S. forces could not train all of the SDF personnel fighting in Raqqa. Instead, the military trained mostly Kurdish SDF unit leaders, who in turn trained the rest of the force—a train-the-trainer model.[27] This approach helped train SDF soldiers more rapidly but reduced direct U.S. visibility and influence over individual SDF fighters.[28] According to one former general officer, "We did not try to get in and try to reorganize the SDF; we didn't try to impact their training and recruiting pipeline."[29]

State Department officials interviewed for this study reported difficulties getting DoD to engage directly with the SDF about the protection of civilians. Overall, according to one official, "it was a challenge to ensure DoD could support efforts to push the SDF to engage the humanitarian community appropriately and in a way that recognized humanitarian principles versus post-conflict political objectives."[30] The training that the coalition provided to the SDF on the "law of armed conflict, ethics, and human rights" took place for only one hour during a two-week training program.[31] According to SOJTF-OIR's plan of instruction, coalition forces provided training on the law of land warfare and armed conflict, protected people, protected places, civilians on the battlefield, and media on the battlefield.[32] Although law of war education is critical, it is insufficient because it does not instill practical civilian-harm considerations that partner militaries need in order to plan and conduct their operations in a manner that mitigates civilian harm; such considerations include understanding how to distinguish targets from civilians, operate equipment responsibly, call in fires, use a CDE methodology, identify structures with civilian functions, use no-strike lists, and more. Partners also need to practically understand how to track civilian harm, analyze incidents of civilian harm for lessons learned, and conduct proper investigations.[33] Because the Counter-ISIS Train and Equip Fund was run by DoD, the Department of State was largely unable to provide inputs to the process of training and equipping the SDF. According to State Department officials, "offers to conduct law of war training or training on humanitarian principles, the importance of access[ing and supporting fleeing populations], and the needs or rights of detained people were largely spurned, ignored, and left unfunded by SDF and DoD until much later in the post-phase of

---

[26] General officer and SOF operator, interview with the authors, July 2020; SOF operator, interview with the authors, February 2020.

[27] DoD official, interview with the authors, March 2020; general officer and SOF operator, interview with the authors, July 2020.

[28] Congressional Research Service, 2017.

[29] Former general officer, interview with the authors, July 2020.

[30] State Department official, interview with the authors, October 2020.

[31] International organization official, interview with the authors, August 2020; general officer and SOF operator, interview with the authors, July 2020.

[32] SOJTF-OIR, "Law of Armed Conflict, Ethics, and Human Rights," LOAC Plan of Instruction, undated (provided to the authors in August 2020).

[33] Lewis and Holewinski, 2013, p. 63.

the Raqqa campaign."[34] According to one State Department official, the Counter-ISIS Train and Equip Fund "was not open for discussion. The attitude from DoD was, 'Don't you know there is a war going on?'"[35]

Despite these shortcomings, multiple senior U.S. military officers emphasized that U.S. forces never questioned the SDF's commitment to mitigating civilian harm, and there were not significant concerns that the SDF would "act in a way that would discredit them or us."[36]

The SDF Required More Air Support to Compensate for Its Lack of Organic Fires and Defenses, Leading to Greater Destruction

With limited equipment from the United States, the SDF was not a heavily armed force that could execute complicated combined-arms maneuvers. Instead, it required a substantial amount of close air support. According to one senior U.S. military official, "the SDF and ISIS were evenly matched on the ground—airpower was what made the difference."[37] As a result, the overwhelming number of fires in support of the SDF were from the air.[38] The SDF preferred to nominate entire buildings as targets for air strikes rather than risk additional casualties breaching the building with its own forces.[39] According to one U.S. pilot who deployed in Raqqa, "the SDF didn't want to breach buildings, so we dropped the entire building. ISIS couldn't shoot from it if it was gone."[40] Another pilot who flew missions over Raqqa concurred, "50 percent of the time, the whole building was getting handed to me as a target."[41]

U.S. operators also reported needing to provide significant air support in collective self-defense of SDF personnel during troops-in-contact scenarios (in other words, when SDF troops were under fire from ISIS). U.S. operators reported that SDF tactics on the ground were different from those of other partner forces they had previously worked with. Specifically, the SDF maneuvered forward aggressively and often needed U.S. airpower to bolster collective self-defense. According to one U.S. operator, "the SDF would move on ISIS fighters very quickly. They'd take losses and keep moving."[42]

As noted in Chapter Six on airpower, dynamic air strikes launched in urban areas as self-defense inherently carry greater risk of causing civilian casualties because of the compressed timeline in which they occur and because pilots have limited visibility into structures. Moreover, targets nominated in self-defense do not need to go through the same sequences of approvals and checks, including a full CDE. As the SDF breached certain neighborhoods in Raqqa, one U.S. operator put the percentage of air strikes taken in self-defense upward

---

[34] State Department official, interview with the authors, October 2020.

[35] State Department officials, interview with the authors, January 2020.

[36] Senior military officers and a retired senior military officer, interview with the authors, July 2020.

[37] General officer, interview with the authors, July 2020.

[38] U.S. Air Force pilot, interview with the authors, April 2020.

[39] Former general officer and U.S. Air Force pilots, interview with the authors, May 2020; U.S. Air Force pilot, interview with the authors, April 2020.

[40] U.S. Air Force pilot, interview with the authors, May 2020.

[41] U.S. Air Force pilot, interview with the authors, April 2020.

[42] U.S. Air Force pilot, interview with the authors, April 2020.

of 70 percent.[43] At times, the SDF pushed U.S. operators to provide air support beyond just collective self-defense and as "shaping fires." In practice, this expansion would have meant that, had ISIS fighters used a road as a line of communication, that road would at some point threaten the SDF, and U.S. forces could strike the road even if it was 20 miles away from an SDF patrol. U.S. operators explained that they turned down SDF requests for shaping fires because the collateral damage to civilians was unknown.[44]

The absence of U.S. forces on the front lines to identify ISIS targets and coordinate strike requests compounded these difficulties. Figure 8.1 provides a simplified illustration of the SDF's role in targeting in Raqqa.

Without certified U.S. JTACs authorized to be on the front lines, SDF fighters were given networked tablets with map software installed (known as Android Tactical Assault Kits), through which U.S. forces could track SDF movements.[45] SOF leveraged high-bandwidth, over-the-horizon communication tools that enabled them to stream full-motion video of the battlefield from multiple sources (including the SDF tablets and coalition ISR) "out of the back of a truck" alongside SDF battalion commanders in order to get a common picture of the battlefield, including the locations of friendly forces, civilians, and ISIS.[46] When the SDF called in an air strike, the tablets enabled U.S. forces to see that, for example, tablet 18 was taking fire from a building 30 yards away. U.S. forces would cross-check and validate this information with U.S. data, including from ISR platforms overhead.[47] According to Eric Oehlerich, a former U.S. SOF operator and planner, "these tools were applied to mitigate risk to the force [and] partner forces and gain a higher level of understanding about civilians in the area in order to avoid CIVCAS [civilian casualties] and preserve the mission."[48] However, communicating through a partner force inherently added a layer of complexity. According to one U.S. pilot,

> If [the U.S. Air Force] was working with our own forces, the pilot could say to ground forces, "move up to this line, you're good to go, I'm going to hit the target." But when we [pilots] aren't in direct communications with the ground force because it's running through a strike cell, or through the embedded [special operations] forces, now it is like playing a game of telephone.[49]

During troops-in-contact situations, U.S. operators reported that it was sometimes difficult to verify SDF targets, given the limited time and ISR assets available, creating a dilemma. According to U.S. operators, the overarching challenge in minimizing civilian harm was

[43] U.S. Air Force pilot, interview with the authors, April 2020.

[44] U.S. Air Force pilot, interview with the authors, April 2020.

[45] Eric Oehlerich, former U.S. SOF operator and planner and co-founder of Lobo Institute, interview with the authors, April 2020; RAND researcher, interview with the authors, April 2020.

[46] U.S. SOF operator, interview with the authors, January 2021.

[47] Eric Oehlerich, former U.S. SOF operator and planner and co-founder of Lobo Institute, interview with the authors, April 2020.

[48] Eric Oehlerich, former U.S. SOF operator and planner and co-founder of Lobo Institute, interview with the authors, April 2020.

[49] U.S. military operator, interview with the authors, April 2020.

Figure 8.1
Simplified Process Map of the SDF's Role in the Targeting Cycle in Raqqa

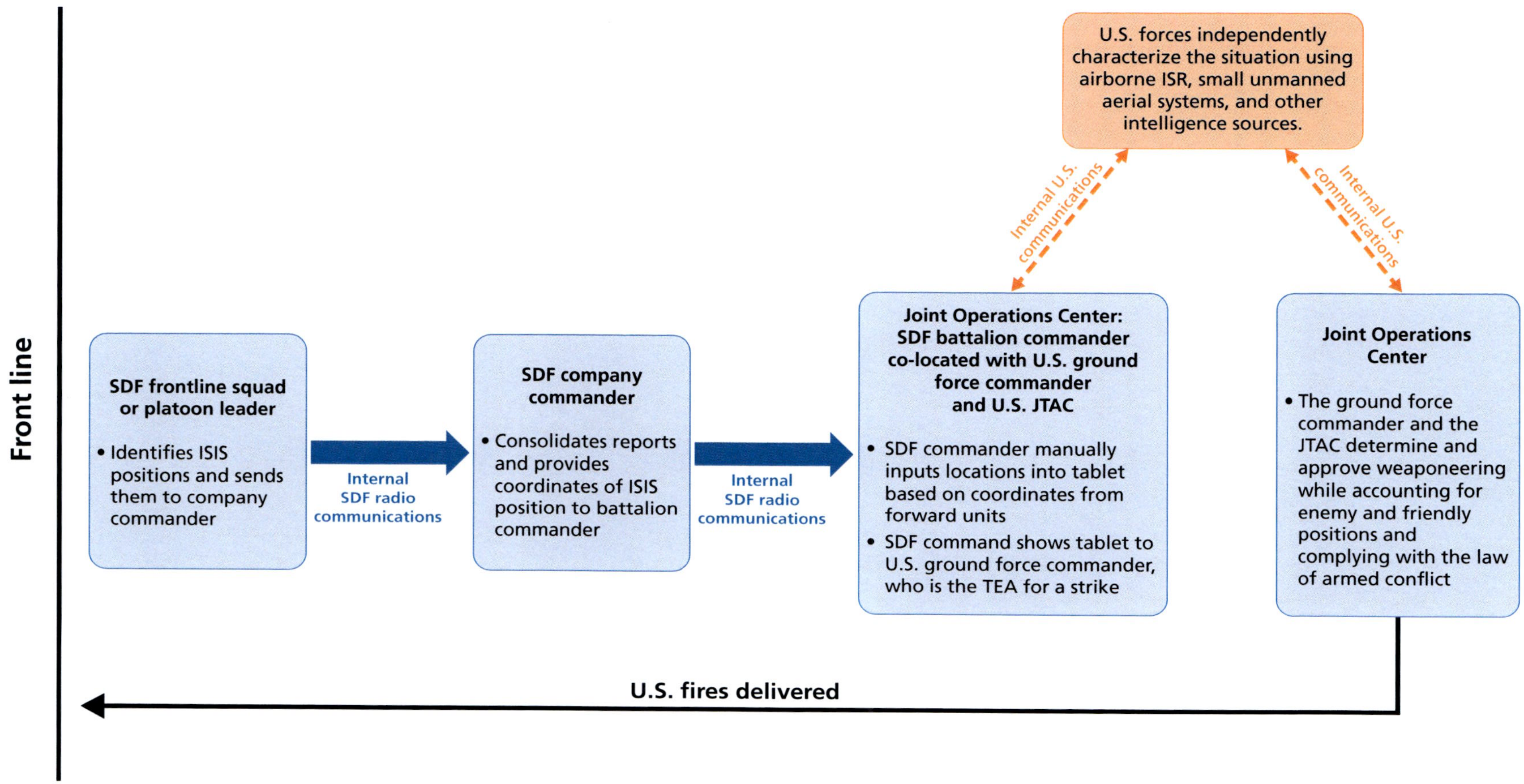

SOURCE: Authors' illustration based on information from a U.S. SOF operator, interview with the authors, January 2021.

achieving a level of certainty about targets. Oehlerich painted a picture of the difficulties operating with partners:

> SDF units are claiming to be in an all-out fire fight and need help now, but they are 50 km away from any American. There is only so much ISR to go around, and you can't do all the same checks you usually would do. If the SDF gets into a TIC [troops in contact], you may not be able to do all that verification because the assets just aren't there.[50]

According to another operator, "You couldn't tell if civilians were hiding in the building. All you knew was that the SDF was there getting chewed up and you are tasked to support them."[51]

Mick Mulroy, former Deputy Assistant Secretary of Defense for the Middle East and former paramilitary officer, stated that keeping U.S. forces at the rear, as opposed to on the front lines where they have better situational awareness and can call in more-precise close air support, can increase the risk of civilian casualties: "If we are going to do this type of partnered operations (and we should be), we need to allow our combat advisers freedom of movement in the battlespace and the commanders latitude on how many personnel they need to accomplish the mission. If not, and we require an arbitrary cap on their number, then we will likely have more civilian casualties."[52] From this perspective, if U.S. operators were closer to the front lines, they might have been better equipped to deal with the self-defense situations through options other than air strikes that leveled buildings. But striking this balance is challenging and involves difficult trade-offs. Several other U.S. officials argued that, if U.S. forces had been on the ground leading operations in Raqqa, there might have paradoxically been more reliance on self-defense strikes to protect U.S. forces than there was to protect the SDF, potentially leading to greater damage.[53]

---

[50] Eric Oehlerich, former U.S. SOF operator and planner and co-founder of Lobo Institute, interview with the authors, April 2020.

[51] U.S. military operator, interview with the authors, April 2020.

[52] Mick Mulroy, former Deputy Assistant Secretary of Defense for the Middle East and retired CIA paramilitary officer in the Special Activities Center, interview with the authors, March 2020.

[53] State Department official, interview with the authors, July 2020; general officer and SOF operator, interview with the authors, July 2020; former general officer, interview with the authors, July 2020; retired senior military officer, interview with the authors, July 2020.

CHAPTER NINE

Civilian-Harm Mitigation Challenges for Intelligence Efforts

In the battle for Raqqa, the coalition faced significant intelligence challenges. Intelligence can be a force multiplier for the warfighter. Prior to operations, it plays a critical role in informing initial situational awareness about a battlespace and contributes to planning targets and mitigating civilian harm. The role that intelligence plays in protecting civilians becomes more complex during fighting, reflecting the dynamic nature of a particular battlefield. The extent to which an intelligence analyst is intimately familiar with an environment can drop and become out of date when an operation begins; obtaining the latest information to maintain situational awareness—even with modern technical capabilities, such as full-motion video, in complement with other intelligence sources—is particularly challenging.[1] Although opportunities for more and improved sources for intelligence collection, analytic tools, and tradecraft exist, the pace of operations will always complicate intelligence efforts to build an accurate and current picture of the environment. Throughout the intelligence cycle, the quality and quantity of intelligence support and the source of intelligence information change, reflecting the availability of information and the pace of operations. Moreover, the number of analysts providing support during active operations is often smaller than that during the preparation stages of an operation. In this chapter, we analyze how intelligence challenges place civilians at risk, especially in urban environments, and how those challenges manifested during the battle for Raqqa.

Some Intelligence Challenges Stemmed from Raqqa's Urban Battlefield

At the start of the battle for Raqqa, the intelligence community's strategic picture of the city and of ISIS was corroborated and robust.[2] The coalition, therefore, started with a fairly good snapshot of the population and city infrastructure in a general sense. However, ISIS's information and physical lockdown of the city limited the extent to which U.S. and coalition forces, as well as SDF partners, could gather insight into a variety of civilian dynamics, including evolving personal relationships, levels of popular support, and patterns of life among the civilian population remaining in Raqqa before and during the battle. Intelligence collection is generally less effective when U.S. forces do not control the battlespace, as was the case in northeastern Syria. Raqqa's urban battlefield compounded these challenges. Generally speaking, intelligence can better prepare an operational force for fighting in a dense urban environment.

---

1 Retired senior military officer, interview with the authors, July 2020.

2 National and defense intelligence officials, interview with the authors, January 2020, February 2020.

Once operations begin, however, the city becomes a dynamic environment: Buildings become fighting positions, the destruction of buildings shifts communication and travel routes, and internally displaced persons move among the fighters.[3] Furthermore, the types and quality of data available from the various intelligence entities differ with each operational phase. Technical collection, including signals intelligence and imagery, can be continuously available but cannot provide the level of detail that human intelligence provides. Human intelligence can be deployed prior to the onset of operations and after forces have seized control of an area and secured it, but such intelligence is not as immediately available during operations, aside from information received from participating soldiers. All of these elements were at play in Raqqa, increasing the "fog of war."[4] Additionally, U.S. operations in the city during the years prior to the battle focused on targeting ISIS senior leaders and those associated with planning and conducting external operations in Europe and the United States, not on building an understanding of the civilian environment.[5] The intelligence required for counterterrorism operations that targeted high-value individuals was significantly different from the intelligence needed to fully understand the human terrain in support of more-conventional military operations.[6]

Relying on a Partner to Provide Intelligence Can Raise Corroboration Concerns

Issues related to relying on a partner force extend to intelligence collection as well. Since September 11, 2001, the U.S. intelligence community has leaned considerably on liaison relationships with host-nation intelligence services to combat the terrorist threat emanating from al-Qa'ida. Over the past two decades, efforts have expanded to counter the threat emanating from other transnational and local terrorist groups. Working with foreign liaisons to counter these threats has several benefits. First, by delegating certain intelligence tasks to foreign liaisons, U.S. intelligence analysts can prioritize scarce U.S. collection resources elsewhere. Second, foreign liaisons can help provide intelligence access to terrorist safe havens, which would not have been accessible to U.S. collectors otherwise. Third, liaisons help U.S. analysts leverage foreign intelligence services' native-language capabilities and cultural awareness.[7]

Liaison relationships exist across all intelligence collection capabilities, although the quantity and quality of contributions made by the various intelligence disciplines differ depending on the operational phase they support. During our research, a former senior U.S. military official we interviewed stated that there was significant concern over a lack of human intelligence during the battle for Raqqa. Having human sources on the ground likely would have provided more insights into the intentions of ISIS fighters and the civilian environment in the city.[8]

[3] Raqqa Study Group, 2018, p. 33.

[4] Senior military officer, interview with the authors, August 2020.

[5] Kogan, 2017, pp. 8, 38, 41.

[6] Senior military officer, interview with the authors, August 2020.

[7] Daniel Byman, "The Intelligence War on Terrorism," *Intelligence and National Security*, Vol. 29, No. 6, 2014; and Jennifer E. Sims, "Foreign Intelligence Liaison: Devils, Deals, and Details," *International Journal of Intelligence and CounterIntelligence*, Vol. 19, No. 2, 2006.

[8] Senior military officers and a retired senior military officer, interview with the authors, July 2020; senior military officer, interview with the authors, August 2020.

The extent to which a liaison relationship could have been established with the SDF also suffered from limitations. First, and as explained earlier, the majority of SDF fighters were not local to Raqqa. Indeed, their status as foreigners in the tribal eastern regions of Syria likely affected the quality of information that they received from local civilians and leaders and limited the SDF's ability to identify reliable sources of information. However, a U.S. operational commander emphasized that the SDF had frequent and strong communication with local leaders before and during the battle.[9] Second, the SDF's intelligence collection tradecraft was likely not of the same quality as U.S. or coalition practices around intelligence collection, which posed a risk to the quality of any information received. These differences could also raise counterintelligence concerns related to the conduct of battle or to U.S. force identification and security.[10] Finally, the establishment of a liaison partnership with the SDF ran the risk of facilitating the extent to which the partner force might have attempted to influence the provision of U.S. support and actions on the battlefield, both operationally during the battle and politically to ensure ongoing support for reconstruction and diplomatic legitimization.[11]

Intelligence Support to Operations and Targeting Generally Focuses on Planning and Mitigation

Multiple guidance documents point to the critical role of intelligence in mitigating civilian harm and casualties during war. Joint Publication 3-60, *Joint Targeting*, not only discusses the joint targeting cycle but also highlights the responsibilities that intelligence personnel have in informing the cycle. The intelligence community coordinates with operational and planning personnel by providing intelligence assessments and products and by managing intelligence collection priorities that characterize the target environment. Part of this support includes participating in the development of targeting packages (beginning with identifying a specific and legitimate potential structure for targeting), contributing to the CDE process, and placing objects on no-strike lists.[12] Target intelligence briefs, target materials, battle damage estimates and assessments, and re-strike or future targeting recommendations are all examples of services that the intelligence community provides to combat operations.[13] All of these products account for the need to mitigate civilian harm.

---

[9] Senior military officers, interview with the authors, July 2020.

[10] Sims, 2006; Gabriel Margolis, "The Lack of HUMINT: A Recurring Intelligence Problem," *Global Security Studies*, Vol. 4, No. 2, Spring 2013; and Adam D. M. Svendsen, "Developing International Intelligence Liaison Against Islamic State: Approaching 'One for All and All for One'?" *International Journal of Intelligence and CounterIntelligence*, Vol. 29, No. 2, 2016.

[11] Daniel Byman, "US Counterterrorism Intelligence Cooperation with the Developing World and Its Limits," *Intelligence and National Security*, Vol. 32, No. 2, 2017.

[12] Joint Publication 3-60, 2018, p. III-9. The no-strike process begins with the identification, characterization, and nomination of no-strike entities. Such entities are defined by category (which includes multiple categories to protect civilians and civilian-related infrastructure); reviewed by the intelligence community; and, once approved, initially placed on the no-strike list by combatant commands. When personnel build a no-strike list for an operation, they must consult functional elements of a staff, such as intelligence personnel, staff judge advocates, civil affairs staff, and coalition liaisons, as appropriate. Combatant commands ensure that no-strike lists are regularly reviewed and updated (Chairman of the Joint Chiefs of Staff Instruction 3160.01C, 2018, pp. C-1, C-2, C-13, B-4).

[13] Joint Publication 3-60, 2018, p. III-10.

Although the joint targeting documents and manuals encourage practitioners to consider how civilians live in the environment, the baseline intelligence assessment does not consider civilians as active elements of an area. At the strategic level, national intelligence analysis and collection priorities focus on foreign intelligence—understanding an adversary's warfighting capabilities, its doctrine, and how decisions are made so that U.S. policymakers can leverage the full toolkit of options against an enemy. Intelligence preparation of the operational environment, a critical element in operational planning, prioritizes analysis of the adversary so that the U.S. military can defeat it. While this preparation step includes requirements to analyze the infrastructure systems and human terrain, the information required is relegated to statistics about ethnicity, economic class, political ideology, and social structures;[14] understanding these elements does not lay the groundwork for mitigating civilian harm. Guidance on the intelligence preparation process does discuss the criticality of infrastructure analysis to support irregular warfare, especially for stability and reconstruction considerations; the extent of infrastructure analysis conducted before the battle is unknown.[15] Moreover, the process does not emphasize the idea that an area of operations is a dynamic and living space that civilians will continue to move within during a battle, thus requiring vigilant intelligence collection and analysis to mitigate civilian harm.

The intelligence community continues to make ongoing efforts to include open sources of information to inform the analysis of the human terrain. For example, Oak Ridge National Laboratory's population density tables and LandScan efforts incorporate data from official government sources and modeling on building functions and how buildings are generally occupied in an area.[16] The identification of potential target entities and the development of deliberate target packages leveraged this information prior to the battle for Raqqa.[17]

However, the ability of these programs to provide real-time updates on the status of a local civilian population remains limited to nonexistent.[18] The Defense Intelligence Agency (DIA), in collaboration with the broader defense intelligence enterprise and the combatant commands, is currently modernizing the Modernized Integrated Database that analysts and operators reference when building target packages and no-strike lists.[19] DIA is also leading

---

14 Joint Publication 2-01.3, *Joint Intelligence Preparation of the Operational Environment*, Washington, D.C.: Joint Chiefs of Staff, May 21, 2014, p. III-40.

15 Joint Publication 2-01.3, 2014, p. VII-8.

16 The population density tables support the requirement for combatant commands to incorporate demographic data in order to support operational planning and execution, as stated in Chairman of the Joint Chiefs of Staff Instructions 3160.01C and 3370.01B (Oak Ridge National Laboratory, "Population Density Tables," presentation, June 2020b). Communications with a CENTCOM officer confirmed that population density tables are integral elements in the advanced target development phase (the final characterization phases leading to effective target engagement) and CDE (CENTCOM targeting officer, email correspondence with the authors, June 2020).

17 U.S. military targeting officer, email correspondence with the authors, June 2020.

18 Oak Ridge National Laboratory officials, interview with the authors, June 2020; Oak Ridge National Laboratory, 2020b; Oak Ridge National Laboratory, "LandScan Program Overview," presentation, June 2020a.

19 Defense intelligence official, interview with the authors, July 2020. The Modernized Integrated Database is the national-level repository for the general military intelligence available to the entire DoD Intelligence Information System community and to tactical units. Entity-level target development data for all target types are included in the database and accessed by intelligence analysts and targeting professionals who are conducting target development assessments and CDEs or building a no-strike list or restricted target list (Joint Chiefs of Staff, *DoD Dictionary of Military and Associated Terms*, Washington, D.C., June 2020b; and Chairman of the Joint Chiefs of Staff Instruction 3370.01B, 2016).

efforts to collect OSINT and publicly available information (PAI) for the defense intelligence enterprise, and those efforts include developing tools to better integrate OSINT and PAI into all intelligence analysis.[20] OSINT and PAI still comprise critical intelligence sources that improve operators' understanding of the human environment and help protect civilians, thanks in large part to the speed at which the information could be gathered and disseminated to operators. Nevertheless, keeping pace with operations is still a significant challenge.[21] Intelligence did provide operational forces with OSINT and PAI during the Raqqa battle, but it remains unclear the effect that this information had on informing the operational forces' understanding of the human terrain in the city.[22]

Changing from Deliberate to Dynamic Operations Shifted Intelligence Support

A critical contribution of intelligence to targeting operations occurs during the target development phase, in which planners consider specific steps to mitigate civilian harm. As a result, intelligence plays a more significant role when supporting planned, deliberate targeting operations as opposed to targeting operations conducted in fast-moving self-defense situations, which apply a different set of ROE. Deliberate targeting efforts benefit from detailed planning, which allows for thorough review of targets against information available across the intelligence community prior to including the targeting in operational plans. Some dynamic targeting operations also pull from this developed and approved set of targets.[23] However, dynamic targeting can occur during a battle in response to requests to support collective self-defense.

As established in Chapter Six on airpower, the overwhelming majority of strikes conducted in Raqqa were under the collective self-defense ROE to protect and support partners on the ground. Although operating forces continually consult intelligence prior to strikes using these ROE, the time frame for review and consultation is significantly reduced, especially compared with the deliberate targeting process. As the battlefield changes and front lines shift, it can also be difficult to precisely discern the status of civilians in the area. Despite these challenges, TEA, ground force commanders, lawyers, and the intelligence community (among others) make decisions and recommendations based on the best information available to them at the time prior to launching strikes in dynamic environments. For this reason, they require information collection and dissemination tools that are as robust as possible.

---

20 Defense intelligence officials, interview with the authors, June 2020, July 2020. PAI is information that has been published or broadcast for public consumption, is available on request to the public, is accessible online or otherwise to the public, is available to the public by subscription or purchase, could be seen or heard by a casual observer, is made available at a meeting open to the public, or is obtained by visiting a place or attending an event that is open to the public (DoD Directive 3115.18, *DoD Access to and Use of Publicly Available Information (PAI)*, Washington, D.C.: U.S. Department of Defense, August 20, 2020).

21 Karl Haigler, "Guide to Intelligence Support for Military Operations," *The Intelligencer: Journal of U.S. Intelligence Studies*," Vol. 19, No. 1, Spring/Winter 2012.

22 Military intelligence warrant officer, email correspondence with the authors, October 2020.

23 Defense intelligence officials, interview with the authors, February 2020.

Active Operations and ISIS Control of the Information Environment Complicated Real-Time Intelligence Collection

As discussed in Chapter Four, coalition and partner forces were aware of ISIS defensive measures prior to the start of the battle for Raqqa. Despite knowledge of ISIS deception measures, such as the use of tarps, tunnels, and holes between buildings to facilitate movement without being detected by coalition ISR assets, having this knowledge beforehand did not make the conduct of operations easier. For example, despite its availability, full-motion video technology was unable to see underground, through tarps, or through walls.[24] A senior U.S. military official noted that current collection efforts are biased in favor of air-to-ground collection versus on-the-ground collection sources.[25] Therefore, although full-motion video generally can provide insights into understanding civilian patterns of life, ISIS defensive measures complicated the utility of that tool before and during the battle for Raqqa.

Similar intelligence challenges stemmed from ISIS's control of the information environment, as the group significantly restricted access to the internet and cell phone networks not only in Raqqa, but throughout the territory they controlled.[26] In an era when almost everyone has a smart phone and social media access, human beings produce excessive quantities of PAI that can support understanding of the human terrain in a nearly real-time capacity. For example, one general officer described that, during the same time frame of the battle in 2017, his staff built a common operational picture of pro–Syrian regime and pro-Russia force locations in southeastern Syria based on PAI, which was "extremely reliable."[27] Limited OSINT and PAI collection, combined with the other challenges, increased the potential for civilian harm in Raqqa.

In addition, ISIS was able to leverage the urban environment during the battle to its advantage; from the intelligence perspective, this complicated efforts to leverage all sources of intelligence collection to support operations and understand the human terrain. Although thorough planning and intelligence collection prepares U.S. forces for what the civilian landscape will potentially look like, troops-in-contact scenarios change the situation significantly and rapidly, including dynamics surrounding the movement of civilians across the battlespace. Even if ISIS fighters had not used methods to obscure their battlefield movements in Raqqa, including using civilians and civilian structures as shields, U.S. ground forces and SDF fighters involved in active operations knew more about the battlespace than did intelligence analysts and collectors, even those monitoring ISR feeds. Although full-motion video can provide insights into one facet of the state of play, it is not infallible.[28] One senior U.S. military official noted that, during the battle for Raqqa, more human intelligence would have been essential to better understand the city's civilian landscape; the interview highlighted his professional experience of the limitations of ISR for truly being able to establish pattern of life.[29]

---

[24] Raqqa Study Group, 2018, p. 34; defense intelligence officials, interview with the authors, January 2020; senior military officers, interview with the authors, July 2020; Dillon and Stump, 2017; Ryan Dillon and Eric J. Pahon, "Department of Defense Press Briefing by Colonel Dillon via Teleconference from Baghdad, Iraq," transcript, U.S. Department of Defense, September 7, 2017; and Salma Abdelaziz, Nick Paton Walsh, and Mohammad Eyad Kourdi, "Raqqa: Secret Video Shows ISIS Losing Chokehold on Its 'Capital,'" CNN, June 27, 2017.

[25] Senior military officer, interview with the authors, August 2020.

[26] SecDev Foundation, "ISIS Steps Up Information Control in Raqqa and Deir Ezzor," *Flash Notes*, Vol. 5, August 5, 2015.

[27] General officer, interview with the authors, August 2020.

[28] Margolis, 2013; senior military officer, interview with the authors, August 2020.

[29] Senior military officers and a retired senior military officer, interview with the authors, July 2020.

CHAPTER TEN

Challenges Identifying, Reporting, and Investigating Civilian Harm in Raqqa

Assessing the extent and nature of civilian harm in the aftermath of military operations is critical for establishing feedback loops to assist the U.S. military in reducing civilian harm and improving mission effectiveness in future operations. Assessments and investigations of civilian harm also demonstrate transparency and accountability on the part of the U.S. military, give the U.S. government and public a better ability to consider the costs of war, and are part of the U.S. commitment to monitor its compliance with the law of war.[1] During the Raqqa operation, CJTF-OIR had a process through which it assessed information indicating that civilian harm may have resulted from coalition operations, which we describe in this chapter. NGOs and international organizations also attempted to take stock of civilian harm in Raqqa during and after the operations. As we demonstrate in this chapter, several factors made it difficult to definitively account for civilian harm in Raqqa.

CJTF-OIR's Policy for Assessing and Investigating Civilian Harm in Raqqa

The CJTF-OIR civilian casualty cell (CIVCAS cell) was responsible for receiving all reports of civilian casualties in Raqqa (and OIR more broadly) and assessing their cause. CJTF-OIR's process for assessing a civilian casualty event begins with a first impression report, which must be sent to the cell within 24 hours of awareness of an incident for which there is information that civilian casualties may have resulted from coalition operations.[2] A report of possible civilian casualties may be raised by NGOs, local residents, or U.S. or coalition members (self-report) either upon the completion of an operation or from scanning open sources of information, such as social media. After receiving the first impression report, the cell will conduct an initial assessment to determine whether the date, time, and place of the reported incident matches coalition strike data. The cell will examine coalition records and recommend

[1] An *assessment* focuses primarily on determining whether civilian harm has occurred, but a commander or other DoD official may direct a more extensive *investigation* to obtain additional facts about the incident through an appointing order. Investigations focus on specific questions as defined in the appointing order—for example, to better understand causal factors and identify process improvements or other recommendations to reduce the risk of future civilian harm. Although different DoD components can have different investigation procedures (e.g., in an Air Force commander-directed investigation or an investigation subject to the Navy and Marine Corps Manual of the Judge Advocate General), Army Regulation 15-6 investigations are the most commonly used in recent joint operations.

[2] The process described in this paragraph is laid out in CJTF-OIR, *Combined Joint Task Force – Operation Inherent Resolve (CJTF-OIR) Policy for Reporting and Responding to Civilian Casualty Incidents*, Camp Arifjan, Kuwait, May 9, 2018.

whether additional inquiry should be conducted through a CIVCAS credibility assessment report (CCAR). According to CJTF-OIR policy, an initial assessment would not recommend a CCAR under three conditions: if no coalition strikes correlate to the area of the reported civilian casualty, if the report provides insufficient information to identify a location or date, or if a partner force or host nation conducted the only strikes correlating to the incident report. If these circumstances do not exist, a CCAR is initiated that provides CJTF-OIR's assessment of whether civilian casualties more likely than not resulted from coalition operations.

The CCAR contains a narrative description of the incident and includes information—such as corresponding coalition strike activity, a CDE, chat logs, full-motion video, and PAI—to support its conclusions. A legal adviser also reviews the CCAR to ensure that sufficient information has been provided to support the findings and to assess whether the strike complied with the ROE and law of war. A report of potential civilian casualties is deemed *credible* based on a standard of *preponderance of evidence*—a determination that it is more likely than not (at least a 51 percent probability) that the coalition is responsible for the civilian casualty. A CCAR is meant to provide an appraisal of information and identify key facts related to the incident, but it is not a full, administrative investigation. According to CJTF-OIR's policy, an administrative investigation, conducted in accordance with Army Regulation 15-6 or other service equivalent, shall be conducted if it is determined that further information is needed to document the underlying facts of the incident or to answer questions not fully addressed by the CCAR. Commanders may also initiate a preliminary inquiry or full investigation (generally under Army Regulation 15-6 provisions) into the incident at any time.

Civil Society's Approach to Assessing Civilian Harm in Raqqa

The military and NGOs have different sources and methods for identifying and verifying incidents of civilian harm. These differing methodologies can create friction during the civilian casualty assessment process. The U.S. military, as described earlier, relies primarily on operational data (e.g., records of whether the military conducted an operation in a given location on a given day), intelligence reporting, overhead imagery, information from ground forces (where available), information submitted to DoD by members of the public, and other available information.

In contrast, NGOs conduct open-source conflict monitoring; leverage local news, social media sites, and YouTube footage of incidents; and conduct in-person interviews with victims, witnesses, medical personnel, local authorities, or community leaders to understand and verify reports of civilian harm.[3] The NGO Airwars aggregated local media and social media reports of civilian harm in Raqqa and sometimes exchanges information with CJTF-OIR to assess evidence of specific civilian-harm incidents. International organizations, including the United Nations International Children's Emergency Fund, also leveraged their networks in Syria to

---

[3] For more information on the methodologies of these three organizations, see Amnesty International, *"I Won't Forget This Carnage": Civilians Trapped in the Battle for Raqqa – Syria*, London, 2017, p. 8; Ole Solvang and Nadim Houry, *All Feasible Precautions? Civilian Casualties in Anti-ISIS Coalition Airstrikes in Syria*, New York: Human Rights Watch, September 24, 2017; and United Nations Assistance Mission in Afghanistan, *Afghanistan: Protection of Civilians in Armed Conflict—First Quarter Report: 1 January–31 March 2020*, Kabul, April 2020, p. 8.

provide data on civilian harm to SOJTF-OIR.[4] According to NGO officials, Raqqa was one of the "cleanest" post-combat environments to study civilian casualties.[5] NGO officials noted that it was easier to determine civilian casualty estimates in Raqqa because of three factors. First, the division of labor in the operation was clear: SDF fighters were on the ground, and coalition forces were providing all aerial and artillery fires. Second, all artillery strikes and 95 percent of air strikes were taken by U.S. forces, which meant that it was almost always possible to determine who the responsible party was for a civilian casualty based on the type of munition used. Third, U.S.-backed forces captured Raqqa and ISIS forces left, so it was possible for researchers and journalists to visit the city directly after it was captured. As we discussed in Chapter Four, different assessment methodologies produced different conclusions regarding the extent of civilian harm in Raqqa.

Challenges with Assessing and Investigating Civilian Harm in Raqqa

Several factors explain why assessments of civilian harm by CJTF-OIR were challenging in Raqqa. First, the use of airpower in support of ground operations led by the SDF dominated the Raqqa operation. Aerial surveillance cannot easily detect incidents of civilian harm, especially when civilians are hidden in structures or in canyons of urban terrain. For example, one study identified that, during U.S. military operations in Afghanistan in 2010, air-video battle damage assessments missed civilian casualties that were later discovered during ground-led investigations in 19 of 21 cases—more than 90 percent of the time.[6] Large-scale ground operations led by U.S. forces, by contrast, have inherent advantages when it comes to detecting when civilian casualties have occurred. In U.S. operations in Afghanistan and Iraq during Operation Enduring Freedom and Operation Iraqi Freedom, for example, ground forces served as sensors to reveal and more precisely discern civilian harm. In Raqqa, U.S. forces relied heavily on ISR assets to assess civilian harm caused by U.S. strikes. However, ISR is inherently limited in the kind of information it can collect, especially in urban operations.[7] For example, full-motion video cannot record damage that occurs below an opaque surface, such as a collapsed roof. Human remains buried in the rubble of a building's basement struck by a U.S. air strike would likely remain undetectable. This detection problem was particularly pernicious in Raqqa, where the United Nations Institute for Training and Research estimated that 11,000 total structures were damaged or destroyed during the operation, although this estimate does not attribute all of this destruction to U.S. or coalition forces. Relatedly, U.S. operators in Raqqa noted that CDE scans were highly challenged because targeting pods and ISR assets could not see inside the many buildings that made up Raqqa's dense urban landscape.[8] Moreover, ISR assets were in extremely high demand during the Raqqa operation and in OIR more broadly. As one U.S. operator explained, ISR assets were spread very thin and were retained by

---

[4] International organization official, interview with the authors, August 2020.

[5] NGO official with field experience investigating civilian casualties, interview with the authors, August 6, 2020.

[6] Christopher D. Kolenda, Rachel Reid, Chris Rogers, and Marte Retzius, *The Strategic Costs of Civilian Harm: Applying Lessons from Afghanistan to Current and Future Conflicts*, New York: Open Society Foundations, June 2016, p. 22.

[7] Senior military officers and a retired senior military officer, interview with the authors, July 2020.

[8] General officers and U.S. Air Force pilots, interview with the authors, May 2020.

a patchwork of various entities in support of many different missions.[9] Operators used assets for pre-strike analysis for target development, partner force tracking, positive identification, close air support, and combat assessment. Often, the allocation process for scarce assets prioritized a ground force commander's immediate needs (e.g., close air support), leaving few assets available to source missions that could support the assessment of civilian harm post-strike.[10]

Second, documenting and reporting harm at its source was challenging in Raqqa. Residents in Raqqa were unable to report instances of civilian harm to the coalition. ISIS imposed a media blackout on the city, which would have made it difficult for residents to take pictures and videos of civilian harm.[11] Even if residents were able to document evidence of civilian harm, it was not clear how or to whom they should submit this information to. There was no expectation of recourse or knowledge that reporting civilian harm to the coalition was even possible, and many residents did not feel it was worth reporting such instances.[12]

Moreover, in Raqqa, the coalition did not conduct in-person site visits or interview witnesses to collect more information about civilian casualty incidents, and it did not leverage its partner force, the SDF, to detect civilian casualties that may have occurred. Site visits are time- and resource-intensive and can involve significant risk to the military forces and supporting elements tasked to visit a site. For example, an Army Regulation 15-6 investigation following an alleged civilian casualty incident in Mosul, Iraq, in 2017 included two site visits. During the first, U.S. personnel visited the structure located 450 m from ISIS fighters and had to rapidly egress the area because of security concerns soon after arriving.[13] On the second visit, the investigation team brought two military explosive teams to extract chemical and structural evidence from the site and to take in-depth photos to inform modeling of the structure for in-depth analysis of causation.[14] The team used this evidence to complete forensic analysis of the explosives involved and to create models of weapon effects, identify modes of structural failure, and develop a chain of causation.[15] The team also conducted a series of in-person and phone interviews with Iraqi neighborhood residents, family members, first responders (Mosul Civil Defense), and Iraqi Security Forces. According to a senior U.S. official involved in the investigation,

> It was very valuable to visit the site in-person. Our interviews with the families of the two houses that were destroyed were important to understand what happened. But it was very hard. We needed a U.S. armored convoy, an Iraqi Counter-Terrorism Service escort force, the leadership of a general officer, and the full support of our coalition land component commander to complete the two site visits.[16]

---

[9] U.S. military operator, interview with the authors, April 2020.

[10] U.S. general officer, interview with the authors, May 2020.

[11] Anne Barnard, "U.S.-Backed Forces Begin Assault on Raqqa, ISIS Stronghold in Syria, " *New York Times,* June 6, 2017; and Zaman al-Wasl, "Free Euphrates: Breaking the Media Blackout in ISIS' Raqqa," *Syrian Observer*, May 15, 2017.

[12] U.S. journalist with previous experience reporting on OIR, interview with the authors, June 2020.

[13] U.S. general officer, interview with the authors, May 2020.

[14] U.S. general officer, interview with the authors, May 2020.

[15] U.S. general officer, interview with the authors, May 2020.

[16] U.S. general officer, interview with the authors, May 2020.

An investigation of this scale would have been quite difficult in Raqqa, where the U.S. ground presence was limited to a few hundred SOF operators and the U.S. military did not have a host government to work with. That being said, local reporting estimates that 35 percent of the city was liberated in the first month of the offensive,[17] and ISIS fighters quickly ceded territory to withdraw into the more densely populated city center. With approximately one-third of assessed civilian casualties occurring in the first month of operations, the U.S. military might have considered field investigations to the sites of strikes in those areas.[18] However, the military would have needed to balance this with the need to continue its mission in Raqqa, as the same people and resources that might have been used for investigations may have also been needed for the military mission. U.S. forces might also have leveraged the SDF to provide on-the-ground information on post-strike civilian harm. In Afghanistan, there was a system developed over several years so that Afghan forces could provide information to the United States and the International Security Assistance Force on civilian casualty incidents.[19] Such an arrangement in Syria may have been challenging: Using a nonstate partner force with different priorities, incentives, and biases to conduct post-strike assessments can raise concerns about the quality and integrity of the information. Nevertheless, even if information provided by the SDF was incomplete or imperfect, its veracity could have been judged during the civilian casualty assessment process.

Third, DoD's systems and practices for managing data and records critical to civilian-harm assessments were flawed. Records of operational data are critical to conducting accurate assessments of civilian harm. As described earlier, the CJTF-OIR CIVCAS cell would take reports of civilian casualties that may have occurred and compare the details to operational records of corroborating strikes or actions. But nomenclature surrounding the terms *strike*, *engagement*, and *munition*—as described in the methodology discussion in Chapter One—caused confusion even at the CIVCAS cell. For example, such confusion, combined with the lack of a common operational picture approach for headquarters staff, led a public affairs officer to incorrectly say that the coalition had not conducted strikes in locations that a *New York Times* reporter had asked about.[20]

In addition to challenges created by a lack of understanding around terminology, records themselves could be incomplete or inaccurate. According to one U.S. operator, "I know from experience that data is missing, but I can't tell you how much."[21] The source of error in the military's records is likely severalfold. First, records of strikes are not automatically recorded in every case; sometimes, they are manually reported from the command executing the strike and typed by hand into a strike log, where they are subject to human error. Second, during the CCAR process, there are challenges to finding the best supporting information, including a lack of clarity surrounding which component to task for the information. For example, CJTF-OIR procedures direct the CIVCAS cell to send the request for information to whomever authorized the strike, but according to one U.S. operator, the air unit conducting or

[17] Syrian Observatory for Human Rights, 2017.

[18] The one-third figure is based on assessed civilian casualties from CJTF-OIR's monthly civilian casualty reports, which CJTF-OIR provided to the authors.

[19] NGO official, interview with the authors, August 2020.

[20] Former U.S. military officer, correspondence with the authors, September 2020.

[21] Operational command staff, interview with the authors, June 2020.

supporting the strike often has better data. In another example, the official battle damage assessment for strikes in the CJTF-OIR area of operations was located on a classified network that some individuals in the CIVCAS cell could not access. Finally, the military does not always archive and preserve the data it needs for civilian casualty assessments. For example, during OIR, the analysis tool that stored full-motion video from strikes was replaced with a new system, and one U.S. official had to get on a plane to another country to retrieve a hard copy of the database. Archiving and preserving such a system is critical to having accurate assessments of civilian harm.[22]

Difficulties accessing information were heightened when analyzing strikes that were not planned, deliberate strikes. Pre-planned strikes benefited from a wealth of information, including an intelligence package, planned weaponeering, and CDE, all of which helped the military assess events post-strike. Air strikes taken in self-defense or collective self-defense of partner forces, however, may not have benefited from the same wealth of information. For example, the CJTF-OIR CIVCAS cell often had the most difficulty finding full-motion video and battle damage assessments for self-defense strikes. The frequent rotation of military units also made it difficult to gather quality information on possible civilian casualty incidents that may have occurred months or years prior, because data get lost as people leave and the information does not always remain in theater. Furthermore, information related to civilian casualties is often reported well after an incident. For example, both Amnesty International and Airwars submitted to CJTF-OIR a large amount of information about possible civilian casualty incidents occurring in 2017 in Raqqa, but most of the submissions were not provided until 2019.[23] Without reliable operational data, the military is unable to accurately assess and monitor civilian casualties over time. As previous research has shown, the tracking and analysis of civilian casualties in this manner enable the military to understand the root causes of incidents and address them.[24]

Fourth, personnel assigned to the CJTF-OIR CIVCAS cell received little to no training on the duties that they would be expected to perform, lacked experience dealing with civilian casualties, and sometimes received inadequate guidance. U.S. military personnel assigned to the cell did not receive pre-deployment training on civilian casualties beyond general DoD law of war training.[25] Although billets for the CIVCAS cell are typically coded to ensure that the cells include members with appropriate operational expertise—for instance, field artillery, infantry, joint fires, and intelligence analysis—cell members receive no formal training on the duties that they are expected to execute when they arrive, and learning was mostly "on the job" and "by doing."[26] U.S. operators also reported receiving insufficient guidance on their duties and responsibilities. According to one U.S. operator, the cell could have benefited from additional clarity on "how deep it should dig into each allegation, how much effort it should put

---

[22] Operational command staff, interview with the authors, June 2020.

[23] Operational command staff, interview with the authors, June 2020.

[24] Larry Lewis, *Reducing and Mitigating Civilian Casualties: Enduring Lessons*, Washington, D.C.: Joint and Coalition Operational Analysis, April 12, 2013.

[25] Operational command staff, interview with the authors, June 2020; DoD official, interview with the authors, November 2020.

[26] Operational command staff, interview with the authors, June 2020; CENTCOM officials, interview with the authors, May 2020.

into verifying the reliability of a source, and what to do if there were conflicting cases."[27] For example, after the discovery of a new eyewitness in the midst of an assessment, the CJTF-OIR CIVCAS cell wanted to change its report of how many civilians were killed in an air strike conducted by a non-U.S. coalition partner. The cell could not get guidance through official CENTCOM channels, per guidance documents, and was simply told to "drop it" after three months of work. The lack of training and guidance is compounded because assignments to the cell are typically only one year, so almost no legacy knowledge resides among the staff.[28] According to one NGO official, "once someone was at post for 3–4 months, the quality of interaction increased dramatically."[29]

Fifth, NGOs and international organizations reported difficulty providing inputs to coalition assessments of civilian harm during operations in Raqqa. For example, the United Nations Office for the Coordination of Humanitarian Affairs established the Humanitarian Military Coordination Cell, which served as a liaison to CJTF-OIR and SOJTF-OIR. The cell set up a request for information (RFI) system in which both the United Nations office and the coalition could submit a question related to humanitarian needs in northeast Syria.[30] According to one international organization official, "Most of the RFIs went into a black hole; SOJTF struggled to understand how to respond. Usually the RFIs went to a legal adviser to prepare a response, so either their response was generic, legalistic, or couched in public affairs language, or they provided a request for more information in response."[31] After military operations in Raqqa concluded, a group called the civil military protection working group (which included staff from international organizations, NGOs, CJTF-OIR, and SOJTF-OIR) was established and met monthly in Amman. The working group attempted to establish a relationship with the OIR CIVCAS cell but was blocked.[32] Such an arrangement might have provided a more coherent platform for the various actors in the humanitarian community that were putting forward information on incidents to the coalition for action. This would have enabled the CIVCAS cell, which had limited time and bandwidth, to respond to reports in a more centralized manner.

---

[27] Operational command staff, interview with the authors, June 2020.

[28] CENTCOM officials, interview with the authors, May 2020.

[29] NGO official, interview with the authors, March 2020.

[30] International organization official, interview with the authors, August 2020.

[31] International organization official, interview with the authors, August 2020.

[32] International organization official, interview with the authors, August 2020.

CHAPTER ELEVEN

Findings and Recommendations

Findings

From our research, we developed ten major findings.

U.S. Strategic Choices, Such as the Encirclement of Raqqa, Likely Increased Civilian Harm

To U.S. military operators, Raqqa felt like a perfect storm of unique circumstances that created particularly challenging civilian-harm risks. But on closer look, many of the circumstances—though perhaps unique in their particular details—portend the types of situations that are likely to arise again in the future: ruthless and committed adversaries, high-intensity urban combat environments, and complex geopolitical dilemmas. Some of the circumstances, however, were created by U.S. policy choices—for example, the decisions to limit the number of U.S. ground forces and their proximity to the front line, rely on less-capable partners, and prioritize operations in Iraq. The situation was further exacerbated by gaps in institutional capabilities that the U.S. military has not yet resolved—for example, a lack of prioritization of civilian-harm mitigation during operational planning, gaps in understanding civilian aspects of the operational environment, limitations in how partner forces were prepared to mitigate civilian harm, and challenges in civilian-harm assessment processes. The implications of these choices would be worthy of several studies on their own. Although we focused our study on operational challenges, we also analyzed the civilian-harm implications of one strategic choice—the decision to encircle Raqqa—given the particular relevance it had for some of the operational challenges that followed.

Immediately prior to the Raqqa operation, the U.S. military's strategy in the counter-ISIS fight shifted from shoving ISIS out of safe locations in an attrition fight to encircling and destroying ISIS in its strongholds in order to prevent fighters from escaping the battlefield and moving to new locations in Iraq and Syria.[1] But this shift also drove coalition decisions to avoid creating civilian exit corridors and to drive ISIS deeper into the densely populated heart of Raqqa. The negotiated exit for ISIS fighters in October 2017, which ultimately ended the battle, was led by the SDF with no U.S. involvement; indeed, the United States explicitly and publicly disagreed with the decision.

The strategic decision to encircle ISIS in Raqqa represented a difficult trade-off. By encircling a densely packed, heavily fortified urban city and fighting ISIS without an escape valve or negotiated exit until the very the end of the battle, the coalition put civilians that remained

[1] Jim Garamone, "Mattis, Dunford, McGurk Cite Coalition Progress to Annihilate ISIS," U.S. Department of Defense, May 19, 2017a.

in the city at risk. Allowing an exit corridor—through which some fighters would inevitably escape—may have reduced civilian harm in Raqqa.

At the same time, letting the same ISIS fighters move from one area in Iraq and Syria to the next may have put more civilians at risk in the long run by allowing ISIS to prey on civilians in other areas. It also may have put other campaign objectives at risk, such as stemming ISIS terrorist attacks in Europe and reducing the group's ability to recruit fighters.[2] Policymakers and military officials provided differing assessments of which approach would have struck the right balance. Both arguments have merit, but neither approach was supported with much evidence, and no one appears to have rigorously analyzed the potential implications of the two approaches. In the recommendations section later in this chapter, we describe how modeling these trade-offs may help mitigate civilian harm in future operations.

The Coalition Made Considerable Efforts to Protect Civilian Life, but There Remains Room for Improvement

DoD has policies and procedures at multiple levels that go beyond the law of war to help protect civilians during armed conflict. Nothing we have presented in this report should be interpreted as accusing coalition forces or leaders violating the law of war. During the battle for Raqqa, coalition forces made considerable efforts to protect civilian life within mission parameters. The nature of the conflict in Raqqa and the density of the urban population imposed exceptional challenges on the coalition when it came to mitigating civilian casualties. Civilians were trapped in a dense, urban, active conflict, and, despite efforts to do so, ground forces did not always discern civilians' presence in a building before requesting coalition artillery or air support. Despite robust policies, procedures, and mitigation efforts, coalition forces caused significant civilian casualties and could have prepared and performed better.

Some military operators and commanders we interviewed identified opportunities to better integrate civilian-harm issues into the targeting cycle, and some leaders modeled best practices that we discuss in our recommendations. In Raqqa, U.S. forces faced challenges using targeting tools to reduce civilian harm because of limitations on munitions and ISR, the prevalence of dynamic strikes, inconsistent use of assessments to enhance learning, and heavy reliance on a partner ground force. In many cases, these challenges were overcome through strong leadership and adaptation, but there was clearly room for improvement.

Civilian Casualties in Raqqa Were Not as High as One Might Predict, Given the High Levels of Structural Damage

Civilians were trapped in a dense, urban conflict zone, and it was often extremely challenging for coalition forces to discern civilian presence. However, the high levels of structural damage in Raqqa should have implied a higher civilian casualty rate, if circumstances in Mosul and Aleppo were any indication. In Mosul and Aleppo, there was one building damaged per civilian casualty; in Raqqa, the ratio of structures damaged to civilian casualties was about three to one.

In addition, the rate of civilian casualty incidents in Raqqa was lower than what would otherwise be expected, given the rate of fires during the operation. Several factors may have contributed to these outcomes. The first factor is the shrinking size of the battlespace in

---

[2] DoD-hosted civilian casualties roundtable discussion with NGO officials, March 2020; former SOF operator, interview with the authors, April 2020.

Raqqa. As the rate of munitions employed in the Raqqa operation rose in late August 2017, the number of civilian casualty incidents reported declined until nearly the end of the operation. One reason for this gap may be that ISIS controlled fewer neighborhoods in Raqqa by September 2017, and therefore fewer civilians could be put in harm's way. Second, the steady decline of civilians remaining in Raqqa during the operation indicates that it was possible, albeit difficult, for civilians to leave Raqqa. Coalition forces and the SDF took steps to remove civilians from the city during the operations, and these efforts succeeded despite the coalition's overall strategy for encircling and destroying ISIS in Raqqa. Civilians who fled the city in response to leaflet drops or information operations from the coalition were not permitted to do so within the safety of a formal exit corridor or pause. The exit corridor ultimately negotiated to end the battle likely reduced additional civilian harm but was not planned in advance or approved by the coalition.

ISIS's Defensive Tactics Deliberately Put Civilians in Harm's Way

As the capital of ISIS's so-called caliphate, Raqqa was a particularly high-stakes operation, and ISIS posed significant challenges to the coalition's ability to mitigate civilian harm. Many of the civilian deaths that occurred in Raqqa during the battle to retake the city from ISIS control occurred as a direct result of ISIS tactics that deliberately placed civilians in harm's way. By the time coalition forces advanced to Raqqa, ISIS had become adept at shifting its own tactics in response to U.S. and coalition ROE intended to mitigate harm to civilians. ISIS strategies of deliberately targeting civilians trying to leave the city, purposefully moving around the city with civilians as shields, taking cover in civilian infrastructure, and using canopies to obscure ISR assets designed to spot civilians from the sky created phenomenal challenges for coalition forces and their SDF partners when it came to achieving the dual objectives of retaking the city and protecting its population. More specifically, ISIS snipers were dispersed throughout the city to shoot fleeing civilians, and ISIS embedded suicide bombers to blow themselves up in groups of civilians who tried to leave. Fighters forcibly relocated civilians to areas near their front lines as the coalition offensive progressed, and the fighters rigged buildings with explosives to cause civilian harm that they could then blame on coalition air strikes. Each defensive action that ISIS took in Raqqa increased the likelihood and magnitude of civilian harm.

Extensive Structural Damage in Raqqa Undermined Post-Battle Governing Prospects and Long-Term U.S. Interests

Although coalition forces focused intently on the civilian casualty risk for each strike launched, they largely ignored the impact that the overall campaign would have on civilian livelihoods over the long term. Raqqa endured the most structural damage by density of any city in Syria,[3] and the cumulative effect of coalition strikes significantly contributed to 60 to 80 percent of the city being uninhabitable, according to various estimates.[4]

The extent of the structural damage in Raqqa undermined CJTF-OIR's stated goal of turning over control of Raqqa quickly to the Raqqa Civilian Council and the Raqqa Inter-

---

[3] United Nations Institute for Training and Research, 2017.

[4] As noted in Chapter Four, the United Nations Office for the Coordination of Humanitarian Affairs (2017) estimated that 80 percent of the city was "uninhabitable." Another report on the conditions in Raqqa after the battle, commissioned by the European Union, estimated that the figure was closer to 60 percent of the city. This report was not publicly available, but its findings were shared with us by one of the report writers in an interview with the authors, August 21, 2020.

nal Security Forces. The level of structural damage and the lack of U.S. support for Raqqa's reconstruction led many Raqqa residents to resent the method of their city's liberation.[5] There was very limited U.S. assistance provided for rebuilding the city and preventing ISIS's re-emergence.[6] U.S. stabilization efforts after the battle were repeatedly described by our interviewees as "thin" and failed to effectively coordinate among aid agencies, devote sufficient funding for local governing bodies to facilitate reconstruction, or quickly respond to the urgent need to clear unexploded ordnance from Raqqa following the battle. Local forces and governing bodies faced the challenge of managing Raqqa's reconstruction but lacked the ability or support to carry out this mission.

Airpower Was Not Used to Shape the Battlefield in Raqqa, Which Made Civilian-Harm Mitigation More Difficult

One of the primary obstacles faced by air—and ground—forces working to mitigate civilian harm in Raqqa was the insufficient shaping of the battlefield with deliberate strikes during every phase of the Raqqa operation. Deliberate targeting ahead of the ground maneuver phase helps reduce the resistance that the ground forces face. Our research found little evidence of kinetic shaping and no deliberate targeting beyond the leading edge of the fight in the battle for Raqqa. The practical effect of this approach was that all strikes in Raqqa were dynamic, and it took more dynamic strikes to get through the city. Dynamic air strikes that are launched in urban areas in self-defense of ground forces inherently carry greater risk of civilian harm because of the compressed and urgent timeline in which they occur, and these circumstances limited the situational awareness of coalition forces in Raqqa. Without time for a full CDE, were operators able to identify weaponeering options to reduce collateral damage to structures? Did urgent decisionmaking limit planners' understanding of the importance for civilians of particular structures or infrastructure near targets? Battlefield-shaping operations stopped once the battle transitioned from isolating the city to seizing it, but they should have continued throughout the seizure operation. Deliberate targeting of ISIS capabilities (e.g., command and control, logistics, beddown locations, indirect fire locations) beyond the ISIS forces fighting on the front lines would have reduced ISIS's fighting strength and disrupted its rear area, potentially allowing the coalition to shift the battlespace to less densely populated areas and enabling faster seizure of the city.

The primary limitation of shaping during the seizure of Raqqa was that the coalition lacked an operational-level headquarters for the Raqqa operation to lead deliberate targeting efforts and lacked targeting teams resourced to conduct the intelligence fusion needed for targeting. The slow and protracted process for deliberate strikes, as well as the prioritization of scarce ISR assets to close air support missions, also hampered shaping operations in Raqqa.

Despite these difficulties, air operators made adaptations over the course of the campaign that enabled them to more effectively protect the civilian population of the city. These adaptations included loading fighter jets with a mix of munitions to ensure that pilots were able to choose appropriate weapons for individual air strikes, minimizing the flight time of a weapon so that ISIS fighters would not have the chance to walk into a crowded area where civilians

---

5 Ruth Sherlock, Lama Al-Arian, and Kamiran Sadoun, "'This Is Not Liberation': Life in the Rubble of Raqqa, Syria," NPR, October 26, 2018; Richard Hall, "Raqqa Liberated from ISIS: 'My City Is Now Ruined and Burned Down,'" Public Radio International, October 19, 2017; and Rosenblatt and Kilcullen, 2019.

6 Townsend and Rankine-Galloway, 2017.

were present, and adjusting fusing timers to minimize the amount of fragmentation of the bomb while still meeting the commander's intent for the strike. Increased joint planning and mission rehearsals between air and ground operators may have allowed adaptations like these to take effect earlier in the campaign.

Restrictions on U.S. Ground Forces Made Preventing Civilian Harm More Difficult

Restrictions on the number of U.S. ground forces and the extent to which they could accompany SDF partners compounded many of the challenges already inherent to urban combat. First, precision targeting was particularly difficult for artillery units situated outside the city and called on to provide support to SDF elements operating within the city limits, even when these units used highly specialized guidance kits. As was the case for operators coordinating air strikes, the inability of ground forces to see their targets limited the extent to which they could limit civilian casualties. Second, and relatedly, because U.S. forces lacked a significant ground presence to gain better local knowledge, the enemy's use of specific tactics made isolating ISIS fighters from noncombatants especially difficult. Although sustained information operations targeting the remaining civilians in the lead-up to the Raqqa campaign did help shape the environment to some extent, restrictive authorities over such actions, as well as specific policy decisions, limited the direct involvement of U.S. troops in active combat.

Our research also suggests that operating as a joint force posed some challenges to U.S. ground forces as they worked to mitigate civilian harm. Specifically, ground units involved in the campaign faced frustrations because different services sometimes adhered to different operational cultures on how best to mitigate and respond to civilian harm. What's more, the frequent rotation of conventional ground forces assigned to support the Raqqa campaign caused some messaging and best practices around mitigating and responding to civilian harm to become lost as units moved in and out of the area. In this sense, frequent rotations of USMC units assigned to support SOF contributed to a loss of tempo as seasoned operators left the battlespace and new ones entered. SOF operators have the benefit of staying engaged with a particular area of operations even while on dwell time in the United States, thus reducing any potential losses of tempo, but conventional ground operators from U.S. Army or USMC units often require retraining and acculturation on dynamics unique to a particular area when they first arrive in-country. These dynamics likely complicated the joint force's efforts to maintain consistent messaging around the topic of civilian harm.

Irregular Partner Forces Were Less Precise Than U.S. Forces Would Be and Increased the Risk of Civilian Harm

As an irregular partner force, the SDF provided a much less precise capability, relative to a comparable U.S. force, for defeating a hybrid insurgent-terrorist group like ISIS. By choosing to conduct the Raqqa operation with a very limited ground presence and a high reliance on the SDF, the United States effectively shifted risk from U.S. military personnel to the civilian population of Raqqa.

Indeed, despite the fact that the SDF was a motivated, capable partner in many ways, its forces still contributed to a substantial amount of civilian harm in Raqqa. We found that the SDF took steps to protect civilians before and during the battle for Raqqa, including engaging tribal elders and local leaders about forthcoming military operations and negotiating an exit path for ISIS fighters at the end of the operation to limit harm to civilians still trapped in the city. But, to preserve its limited forces and prevent defection from its fragile coalition of fighters, the SDF appears to have risked greater collateral damage and civilian harm than a comparable U.S. force would have.

The risk of civilian harm posed by this irregular force was increased by three major factors. First, the SDF required more air support to compensate for its lack of organic fires and defenses. Air strikes in dense urban areas launched in self-defense of partner forces carry the greatest risk of civilian casualties because of the compressed timeline in which they occur, the lack of U.S. JTACs on the front lines to provide precise close air support, and potential difficulties verifying partner targets with limited ISR assets and the challenges to discerning the presence of civilians and the proximity of structures and infrastructure on which civilians rely.

Second, U.S. forces did not have command and control over SDF fighters, which put the United States in the position of having to help or sometimes rescue its partners when they got themselves into dangerous situations. Without U.S. ground forces to take and hold territory and to set the pace of operations, the United States ceded substantial control over how much risk the ground force took during the Raqqa operation. In particular, the SDF's tendency to maneuver forward aggressively toward ISIS positions meant that those forces frequently required close air support to assure their self-defense.

And third, the United States trained and advised the SDF on civilian-harm issues to only a limited degree. Time and scale were major constraints in the lead-up to the Raqqa operation, a consequence of the need to quickly identify and support a partner force with a small number of U.S. forces in Syria. Beyond requiring SDF leaders to take a one-hour training session on ethics, human rights, and the law of war, the coalition did not systematically work with the SDF to impart policies and practices on mitigating civilian harm. It also did not conduct planning or develop command guidance that considered the risks to civilians. Furthermore, key players who might have contributed to training and preparing the SDF for the offensive, including the U.S. Department of State and international organizations, were rebuffed.

A Lack of Sources to Provide Better Local Information Impeded Civilian-Harm Mitigation Efforts

The battle for Raqqa provides insights into the future of conflict between the United States and near-peer adversaries, which will likely contain elements of urban warfare. The density and height of buildings in the city provided natural defenses for ISIS, whose fighters manipulated the urban infrastructure to their advantage by constructing tunnels throughout the city. ISIS's reversion to insurgent-type tactics, such as purposely using civilians and civilian objects as shields, often defeated any efforts to collect intelligence via strategic ISR assets. The group's control over the movement of civilians and the information environment in Raqqa also undermined U.S. and SDF efforts to fully characterize the human terrain within the city before and during the battle. If ISIS had not controlled the information environment, including internet and cell phone access, U.S. and coalition forces and the SDF could have had more access to open-source information characterizing movements of the civilian population and changes to the human terrain.[7]

In Raqqa, the intelligence collection apparatus was biased from the top down, relying primarily on air sensors and strategic ISR assets. As discussed earlier, ISIS's physical control of Raqqa and its citizens prevented collection of significant human intelligence—a challenge that

[7] General officer, interview with the authors, August 2020.

multiple U.S. operational and senior military officials highlighted in our interviews.[8] Human intelligence is one method to offset the limitations of airborne collection assets; human sources can often provide better details on the living and changing nature of an area because they are present in the space. Strategic ISR assets additionally focus intelligence and operations on the end state of an operation, defeating the enemy, instead of on building understanding of the human terrain and the civilians living in the environment.[9] When layered with strategic ISR assets, human intelligence can decrease potential issues with positively identifying a target.

In addition, better processes and prioritization could have allowed intelligence analysts to do more to incorporate validated OSINT and PAI into target development, particularly dynamic targeting. More information could have been leveraged remotely if leaders had prioritized intelligence resources to look at city planning information and other open-source data about the locations in which the coalition was operating.

Flawed DoD Processes and Poor Collection of Civilian Casualty Data Hindered the Military's Ability to Assess and Analyze Civilian Harm in Raqqa

In assessing civilian casualties caused by the coalition in Raqqa, the U.S. military relied largely on military operational data and air-based assets to determine whether and how much civilian harm occurred after a strike. As we have documented in this report, both of these sources of data had critical flaws, which prevented the military from recording a comprehensive assessment of civilian harm in the aftermath of the Raqqa operation.

First, the operational data and records that the military used to assess civilian casualty reports were subject to error in numerous ways. For example, some records of strikes were recorded and entered manually, which is subject to human error. Thus, when CJTF-OIR personnel compared the task force's own strike records to the location and time of a civilian casualty report, they might erroneously conclude that CJTF-OIR did not conduct strikes in the area of the alleged incident. In addition, the CIVCAS cell had difficulty accessing the information and evidence that it needed to complete CCARs. For instance, there was confusion around which component possessed the needed data, and some data were stored on decommissioned databases, some were stored on inaccessible networks, and some were lost as military units rotated out of theater. Without reliable operational data, it is very challenging for the military to understand the root causes of civilian casualties, characterize patterns of harm, and identify specific measures that U.S. forces can take to mitigate civilian harm while preserving mission effectiveness and force protection.

Second, aerial surveillance cannot easily detect many incidents of civilian harm, especially in packed urban areas. For instance, full-motion video assets cannot record damage that occurs below an opaque surface, such as a collapsed roof. This detection problem was particularly pernicious in Raqqa, where an estimated 11,000 structures were destroyed during the operation. Civil society organizations with extensive on-the-ground contacts and knowledge might provide information that could help offset the military's relative weakness in this regard, but civil society organizations and Raqqa residents who tried to engage the coalition with their own monitoring data or reporting faced difficulty providing inputs and understanding opaque

[8] Retired senior military officer, interview with the authors, July 2020; senior military officers, interview with the authors, July 2020; senior military officer, interview with the authors, August 2020.

[9] Senior military officer, interview with the authors, August 2020.

military processes.[10] Finally, ground forces (either partner or U.S.) were infrequently leveraged to help fill in information gaps, through either site visits or witness interviews, in what air-based assets could not see. The military may have had legitimate reasons for not leveraging U.S. forces or partner forces to conduct field visits in Raqqa: Such visits are time- and resource-intensive and can involve significant risk, and using a nonstate partner force with different priorities, incentives, and biases to conduct post-strike assessments can raise concerns about the quality and integrity of the information. Nevertheless, the absence of ground forces to act as sensors to reveal civilian harm meant that civilian harm could go undetected or that assumptions that victims were combatants could more easily go unchecked.

Recommendations for Future Improvements

Our findings demonstrate that mitigating and responding to civilian harm are not just operational issues that fall exclusively on the shoulders of commanders and operators on the battlefield. Instead, they are issues that cut across the military as an institution and that should be addressed in decisions related to manning, training, and equipping the entire force; in the joint planning process; and from an operational perspective. Each of these elements provides opportunities to derive best practices around civilian harm so that they become institutionalized across DoD. From our research, we developed eight categories of recommendations that reflect this overarching finding.

Prior to the Start of Military Operations, DoD Must Take a Broader Approach to Civilian Harm That Considers How Strategic Choices Might Affect Civilian-Harm Risks

Raqqa reveals a short-term, narrow approach that DoD took to mitigating civilian harm in the city: Although CJTF-OIR took great care to mitigate risk in individual strike decisions, there were still significant levels of civilian casualties, and the campaign resulted in the destruction of the city, creating a long-term humanitarian disaster for the civilian population. Avoiding such an outcome in the future is partially a matter of designing and shaping operations to better account for civilian protection during the predicted flow of the battle and for the long-term welfare of the civilian population. But this goal could be reinforced by a broader approach to civilian harm that considers the implications of strategic choices, such as the number of U.S. ground forces, restrictions on U.S. ground forces, the air and intelligence resources committed to the operation, the reliance on partners, attrition versus encirclement strategies, the preservation of structures and infrastructure, and other longer-term considerations.

The limited analysis of the trade-offs among attrition, encirclement, or other strategies and the lack of post-operational planning in Raqqa point to the need for strategic analysis that focuses on civilian-harm risks prior to the start of military operations.[11] DoD should consider ways to incorporate civilian-harm mitigation across the joint planning process—including in strategic guidance and mission objectives, course of action development and evaluation, tabletop exercises, wargaming, and modeling and simulation tools—to better understand the implications of DoD strategies through a civilian-harm lens. Specifically, future planning would

[10] Larry Lewis, "Recommendations for Strengthening Civilian Protection," Arlington, Va.: CNA, unpublished working paper, October 2020.

[11] This would be consistent with the concept of the civilian casualty "life cycle" recommended in Sewall and Lewis, 2010.

benefit from a more intensive risk-benefit analysis of confronting enemies in various environments (e.g., urban versus rural), with various types of partners, with various levels of U.S. and coalition air and ground forces, and so forth. For example, wargames might ask participants to assess whether a certain scenario presents joint forces with the opportunity to push or incentivize an enemy out of urban areas prior to encirclement, despite obvious risks.

Furthermore, DoD should work more intensively and at multiple levels with the State Department, the White House, coalition partners, and others to conduct detailed planning and to reserve funding for infrastructure protection and post-battle reconstruction. The Raqqa operation demonstrated a heavy focus on the operational objective of defeating ISIS, but there was a lack of attention to the strategic purpose of restoring stability to the region. The United States should support efforts to remove explosive hazards, reestablish essential services, and secure an area so that civilians can move back into their communities quickly and safely, ultimately empowering them to rebuild their city. This is critical to the long-term success of urban military operations. If civilian officials and military commanders express preservation of infrastructure in their intent, then staffs and targeting planners will execute that intent. If operational design emphasizes the use of deliberate targeting prior to and during ground maneuvers, target planners can use that deliberate targeting in a way that not only maximizes battlefield effectiveness but also mitigates civilian-harm risk. And if more small-yield weapons are available, tactical decisions will not be driven by a commander's intent to preserve such weapons.

These pre-operational plans should also work to strengthen the engagement between the military and humanitarian organizations at multiple levels during multiple points in the operation. DoD officials and military planners should leverage the knowledge these organizations have about the human terrain in particular regions prior to the start of military operations. Doing this in Raqqa would have enabled coalition forces to have a better understanding of anticipated civilian protection issues and the needs and concerns of the humanitarian community. Officials conducting the reconstruction work should also engage the humanitarian community so that a plan to rebuild is well designed and coordinated. The failure to plan for post-operation reconstruction, no matter the level of resourcing, runs the risk of allowing a city like Raqqa to once again become a terrorist safe haven. CENTCOM and CJTF-OIR, along with Iraqi partners, conducted similar planning efforts prior to the battle for Mosul, with positive effects for reconstruction following ISIS's defeat.[12]

Finally, the design of future operations should take into account the tactics and strategies that opponents adopt vis-à-vis local civilian populations. Although popular support is crucial to the organizational survival and strategic success of some armed groups, others prey on civilians and deliberately put them in harm's way to achieve their objectives. Each type of group poses a unique challenge to U.S. forces, and the Raqqa experience with ISIS suggests that U.S. military planners should more deliberately consider how to contend with actors that prey on noncombatant populations and hold those actors accountable for law of war and human rights violations. Some formal mechanisms, such as the 1998 Rome Statute (which created the International Criminal Court), exist to hold belligerents accountable for such harm, but these mechanisms are more likely to deter state aggressors tied into networks of economic interdependence and nonstate groups that seek international legitimacy.[13] Arguably, ISIS falls into

---

12 Retired senior military officer, interview with the authors, July 2020.

13 Hyeran Jo and Beth A. Simmons, "Can the International Criminal Court Deter Atrocity?" *International Organization*, Vol. 70, No. 3, Summer 2016.

neither of these two categories. But other, informal approaches to curbing human rights violations have proven effective and are likely to be advantageous to future U.S. military campaigns against adversaries that deliberately place civilians in harm's way. For example, the practice of naming and shaming states for abuses against their own populations has placed sufficient pressure on some, causing them to change their behavior.[14] Moreover, violent nonstate armed groups that engage in high levels of violence against civilians often suffer from internal divisions that lead to their eventual fragmentation. Although ISIS is a particularly brutal armed group and relatively resilient to these types of information operations, DoD would benefit from considering these activities against other armed groups that might be more vulnerable to targeted and sustained information operations that broadcast law of war violations.[15] In short, there is ample room for U.S. policymakers and the military to harness formal and informal mechanisms to weaken state and nonstate adversaries that rely on civilian abuse as an operational strategy; these should be considered in future combat operations.

DoD Can Improve Its Application of Targeting Processes, Targeting Tools, and Force Preparation

DoD's targeting processes and force preparation efforts were already quite sophisticated leading up to the Raqqa operation. Raqqa's urban setting and the coalition's overwhelming use of dynamic targeting, however, illustrated how much work DoD still needs to do. We identified several best practices and opportunities for improvement in our discussions with U.S. military leaders and operators involved in the effort:

1. Leaders at every level should consider resource requirements from the perspective of civilian-harm mitigation; related resources might include ISR and munitions with low collateral damage.
2. Leaders should utilize every formal and informal means of providing guidance—including planning documents, expressions of commander's intent, and face-to-face discussions—to emphasize the importance of mitigating civilian harm.
3. Leaders should consistently emphasize civilian-harm assessments as learning tools and work to share lessons among units and institutionalize them for future learning.
4. Leaders may find their message more effective when couched in terms of law of war requirements, military professionalism, and mission effectiveness.
5. Training focused on civilian protection issues before and during deployments may help personnel better internalize the importance of civilian-harm mitigation and link it to achieving the overall mission.
6. Considering the targeting cycle through the lens of civilian-harm mitigation may help in the adoption of specific tactics and strategies for ground force commanders, TEAs, JTACs, and other leaders and their teams.
7. TEAs and other leaders should emphasize a culture within their teams that promotes learning from mistakes related to civilian harm and encourages operators to voice concerns regarding the positive identification of targets in the moments before a strike.

---

[14] Cullen S. Hendrix and Wendy H. Wong, "When Is the Pen Truly Mighty? Regime Type and the Efficacy of Naming and Shaming in Curbing Human Rights Abuses," *British Journal of Political Science*, Vol. 43, No. 3, July 2013.

[15] Barak Mendelsohn, "The Battle for Algeria: Explaining Fratricide Among Armed Nonstate Actors," *Studies in Conflict & Terrorism*, 2019.

DoD Should Harness the Considerable Lessons Learned from Raqqa—and from Past Operations—to Better Prepare Ground Forces, Pilots, and Targeting Teams for Future Urban Engagements, Partly Through Improved Education and Training

From an airpower perspective, the experience of the Raqqa offensive suggests that several key investments may minimize civilian harm. First, pre-offensive shaping operations should be prioritized to a greater degree. The opportunity to conduct more-robust pre-offensive shaping operations would benefit not only air operators but also ground forces. Prioritizing expanded shaping operations would significantly help reduce civilian harm resulting from air strikes because it would reduce the extent to which a military force must rely on dynamic strikes, which typically carry greater risk to civilians, during the main offensive. Second, during future urban operations, efforts should be made to ensure that pilots are carrying a sufficient supply of weapons that cause low collateral damage, ultimately improving pilots' ability to tailor weapons to specific targets.

Finally, air operators and commanders would greatly benefit from additional training on urban operations, particularly jointly with ground operators and at the operational level with mission commanders and planners. Military leaders, planners, and operators need opportunities to collaborate on improvements to civilian-harm mitigation in scenarios that may require a lot of dynamic strikes. For example, there may be ways to develop compressed-timeline options for CDE or tools to improve operator awareness of civilian movement and civilian objects in self-defense situations or other dynamic environments.

Although DoD already provides air operators with substantial training on urban operations, the Raqqa campaign provides invaluable insight into the civilian-harm risks associated with future urban warfare operations in other theaters. DoD should harness the considerable lessons learned from this context to better prepare pilots for future urban engagements.

Urban warfare is likely to characterize future conflicts, and ground units must be better trained to operate in such environments in a way that mitigates civilian harm. We offer two recommendations focused on education and training. First, professional military education for officers who will operate in the joint environment, including such elite programs as the Army's School of Advanced Military Studies, should regularly integrate instruction around the complexities of mitigating and responding to civilian harm and should adapt and update instructional modules to ensure that they draw on recent and relevant combat experiences. In May 2020, the Joint Chiefs of Staff issued a new vision and guidance for military education highlighting that the future character of war necessitates a "profound transformation of how the services prepare and educate future leaders at every level."[16] The guidance encourages the use of "live, virtual, constructive, and gaming methodologies with wargames and exercises involving multiple sets and repetitions to develop deeper insight and ingenuity."[17] We also recommend that education rely heavily on historical case study approaches that maximize the potential for effectively implementing lessons learned, given the U.S. military's now-extensive experience dealing with issues of civilian harm. This approach was taken to improve pre-deployment training for forces in Afghanistan, using vignettes built from real-world operations, and this

---

[16] James Lacey, "Finally Getting Serious About Professional Military Education," *War on the Rocks*, May 18, 2020; and Joint Chiefs of Staff, *Developing Today's Joint Officers for Tomorrow's Ways of War: The Joint Chiefs of Staff Vision and Guidance for Professional Military Education & Talent Management*, Washington, D.C., May 1, 2020a.

[17] Joint Chiefs of Staff, 2020a, p. 6.

was one of the more effective means of training.[18] Our research strongly suggests that applying these techniques to improve education on the topic of civilian harm is likely to greatly benefit leaders preparing to operate in a joint environment and, ultimately, DoD's and the joint force's approach to mitigating and responding to civilian-harm incidents.

Second, and relatedly, pre-deployment training cycles should enhance existing law of war and ROE training by building in practical evolutions that expose ground force operators to the complexities that they are likely to face on the battlefield when it comes to mitigating civilian harm. A revised training approach is likely to be most effective if it is led by military personnel who have personal experience dealing with such issues and if it employs vignettes and tactical decision games from recent or ongoing conflicts involving U.S. ground forces. U.S. Army and USMC ground units already train and socialize their troops on the importance of civilian-harm mitigation to U.S. military operations; the continuation and potential expansion of joint training evolutions that expose operators to the complexities of addressing civilian-harm issues in the context of joint operations will further prepare them to be effective warfighters. USMC's large-scale exercises, which can include joint, interagency, and multinational elements, provide a potential launching point for the expansion of such initiatives. Past exercises have included "force-on force, multi-regiment [scenarios] outfitted with significant information operations and UAS [unmanned aerial system] assets."[19] Such exercises provide an opportunity to better train operators from across the services on how to deal with some of the challenges highlighted in this report, including ISR shortages and information operations. In sum, improvements in existing training and education around the law of war that help instill practical skills that aid in mitigating civilian harm during combat will not only further build the situational awareness and confidence of individual operators but also better prepare the joint force to operate more seamlessly when it comes to addressing issues of civilian harm in future conflicts.

An Increased Emphasis on Information Operations Could Reduce Civilian-Harm Risk

U.S. military planners should prioritize information operations, including broadly disseminating messaging that emphasizes the enemy's use of tactics that violate the law of war. Through targeted information campaigns, U.S. forces can play a larger role in de-legitimizing enemy forces, particularly those that share few, if any, ties to local populations and suffer from a lack of popular support. There is a role here for ground planners and operators, as well as for public affairs officers who can broadly disseminate messaging about enemy tactics across a variety of communication platforms.

Finally, evidence from the Raqqa operation suggests that, although SOF have sufficient authorities to conduct information operations to shape an environment, conventional forces may not have such authorities in future operations. The joint force should consider delegating authority over information operations to lower levels—for example, to battalion or squadron commanders, in order to effectively layer information operations into existing policies around mitigating incidents of civilian harm. What's more, information operations can help build trust with local populations, which is important to improving the U.S. military's ability to detect and eventually respond to such incidents when they occur.

---

[18] Lewis, Young, and Messer, 2011.

[19] Philip Athey, "New in 2020: More Gigantic Exercises for the Marine Corps," *Marine Corps Times,* January 21, 2020.

Partnering Efforts Between the United States and Local Forces Should Prioritize Strategies and Tactics to Mitigate Civilian Harm During Military Operations

There are four principal ways in which the United States could help mitigate civilian harm in its partnerships.

First, the United States should perform an assessment of a partner force to identify key capabilities and risks related to civilian harm. At the start of a partnership, DoD officials, in consultation with the Department of State, should assess a partner force's capacity and will to mitigate civilian harm, including its relationship to the civilian population and local community, its security governance and accountability structures, its political considerations and objectives and how they affect civilians, its professionalism and discipline, and its record of integrating international humanitarian law and human rights law into training, operational planning, and ROE.[20] During the Raqqa operation, limitations in the SDF's capabilities and proficiencies, as well as its tolerance for civilian-harm risk, affected the pace of operations and coalition decisions about when and how to provide supporting fire. Assessing and anticipating potential issues arising from partnerships early—especially for partners that are not as relatively capable, motivated, and conscious of civilian-harm issues as the SDF was—will enable the United States to enter the partnership with a clear understanding of the partner's strengths and weaknesses on civilian protection. Such assessments should then inform the types of support the United States provides to the partner.

Second, using the results of that assessment, the United States should take tailored steps prior to the operation to build a partner's capacity and capability on civilian-harm issues. For example, DoD, in consultation with the Department of State, should plan for how it can best leverage a partner's strengths, such as local oversight and accountability institutions, or a partner's access to the local population and knowledge of the cultural context. In addition, DoD should plan for how it can shore up partners' weaknesses. For example, DoD officials might try to formalize civilian protection commitments with local partner forces prior to the start of military operations. The military might document shared expectations between U.S. forces and the local partner regarding how civilian-harm mitigation will be incorporated into training, equipment requirements, joint operations, guidance, and ROE, as well as the response to civilian-harm incidents. For example, after the Raqqa operation, SOJTF-OIR flew senior SDF leaders out of northeast Syria into Iraq to meet with United Nations leaders for a dialogue on civilian protection issues.[21] It would have been beneficial for both the coalition and the SDF if a similar dialogue had been organized prior to the start of operations in Raqqa. In addition, training is an important part of building partner capacity on civilian-harm mitigation prior to military operations. DoD should provide partners with formal training on practices for protecting civilians. A one-hour block of training on the law of war, such as that provided to the SDF, is insufficient. Law of war education is critical, but military forces can comply with the law of war and still harm civilians. More can be done in policy and practice to protect

---

[20] Other researchers have also found that these criteria are important for understanding a partner's ability to protect civilians in conflict (Melissa Dalton, Jenny McAvoy, Daniel Mahanty, Hijab Shah, Kelsey Hampton, and Julie Snyder, *The Protection of Civilians in U.S. Partnered Operations*, Washington, D.C.: Center for Strategic and International Studies, October 20, 2018).

[21] International organization official, interview with the authors, August 2020.

civilians than simply complying with international law.[22] Training should not (and cannot) be designed to bring partner forces up to U.S. standards, but tailoring training to a partner force's observed weaknesses can go a long way in mitigating a partner's gaps. For partners with which the United States has an enduring relationship, advisory efforts are another way to provide continuous training to partner forces, identify patterns, and develop tailored solutions. The U.S. military has employed advisory capabilities to advance civilian protection in various countries, including Afghanistan and Saudi Arabia, and further effort can be made to bolster U.S. advisory approaches to help such partners mitigate civilian harm.[23]

Third, the United States can provide operational support to partners throughout a military operation. DoD should plan to tailor its operational support to address a partner's risks and leverage its strengths. For example, in Raqqa, the military performed certain checks to verify SDF targets before approving strikes. Other types of operational support to partners might include assisting with CDE, leveraging U.S. ISR assets to help a partner with targeting, and providing partners with weapons that are effective in close combat situations to avoid air strikes on buildings.

Fourth, DoD should collect information regarding instances of civilian harm caused by partner forces to avoid accountability gaps. As we noted in Chapter Seven, the United States did not collect information on instances of civilian harm caused by the SDF in Raqqa and does not typically do so with other partner forces. This can lead to an accountability gap because harm caused by local forces—who might be armed, trained, or supported by the United States—cannot be identified or mitigated. Understanding how U.S. partners are using U.S.-supplied weapons, training, and support is critical to informed policymaking. DoD, in coordination with other U.S. government agencies, should establish clear guidance on the responsibilities of U.S. military forces and other U.S. personnel in monitoring the conduct of partners. Where feasible, the military should also consider establishing a process for gathering information on partner units and civilian harm, including how assistance is being used by partners in combat operations. The U.S. government could leverage three sources of information for this "operational end-use monitoring."[24] First, DoD can leverage information from partners themselves—for example, on the location of the strikes, the type of weapon used, or the intended target. Although access is not guaranteed, there is precedent for partners sharing this type of data when the United States specifically requests such details.[25] Second, DoD can leverage U.S. government information, including intelligence that could provide information about what partners are doing on the ground. This would have been difficult in Raqqa, where there was limited human intelligence, but it could be useful in other contexts. Finally, DoD could leverage open-source information, such as that from civil society organizations, social media, city planning documents, and other PAI. Open-source information provides critical insights that complement other sources of military ISR.

---

22 Larry Lewis, "Improving Policy and Practice to Protect Civilians: A Lifecycle Approach," Arlington, Va.: CNA, unpublished working paper, undated-a.

23 General officer, interview with the authors, March 2020; NGO official, interview with the authors, August 2020.

24 Larry Lewis, *Promoting Civilian Protection During Security Assistance: Learning from Yemen*, Arlington, Va.: CNA, May 2019.

25 Lewis, 2019, p. 29.

The U.S. Military and Intelligence Community Should Investigate Opportunities to Develop Tools and Practices That Improve Understanding of the Civilian Environment and Better Leverage Open-Source Intelligence, Publicly Available Information, and Human Intelligence

Intelligence remains critical to supporting a battlefield commander's situational awareness and planning efforts to mitigate civilian harm during operations. It would be nearly impossible to gain perfect situational awareness in a dynamic environment, but we have two recommendations for how to improve collection efforts. First, while recognizing the complexity and time involved, we recommend increasing human intelligence networks. Moreover, collection requirements should be submitted to provide fidelity on the civilian population density, dynamics, and demographics, as well as structures and infrastructure that are important to the health, safety, and well-being of the civilian population. Human intelligence remains a critical element of all-source intelligence analysis, and its inclusion will only improve understanding of an operational environment.

Second, we recommend that DoD increase efforts to better incorporate validated OSINT and PAI into the target development process, particularly dynamic targeting. DoD Instruction 3115.12 established the DoD Open Source Council as "the primary governance mechanism for DoD OSINT."[26] In addition, the Open Source Intelligence Center was established within DIA to consolidate DoD OSINT collection activities and thus ensure that activities and resources are efficient and that the correct information is being collected to fill defense intelligence requests.[27] DIA's ongoing process of updating the Modernized Integrated Database has developed PAI data-scraping tools to ingest open-source information, making it available to analysts who are developing target packages. Similarly, command-level OSINT capabilities need to be better harnessed to support deliberate and dynamic operations. We recommend that these processes for defense intelligence OSINT collection and tool development continue. DIA should consult with targeteers, operational commanders, and combatant commands to ensure the inclusion of PAI sources that reflect the movement of civilians and the identification and use of civilian structures. The intelligence community, DoD, and combatant commands must expect that near-peer competitors are likely to control and influence the information environment similar to how ISIS did, and OSINT and PAI collection efforts and tradecraft must address these potential credibility issues.

Despite the focus on collecting OSINT and PAI, a gap exists in analytic tradecraft and analysis training specifically related to those sources of information. In addition to establishing the Open Source Intelligence Center, DIA has investigated how to include data scientists in the agency. Initially a de facto recognition of a weakness, the hiring of data scientists can support analytic tradecraft on sorting, organizing, and assessing the validity of the massive quantities of PAI.[28] OSINT will complement all-source target development and assessment analysis and will be critical to understanding the dynamic human terrain. Since the publication of a 2016 RAND report on data science functions in the agency, DIA has taken steps to

---

[26] DoD Instruction 3115.12, *Open Source Intelligence (OSINT)*, Washington, D.C.: U.S. Department of Defense, July 16, 2020, Enclosure 3, p. 11. For more information, see Heather J. Williams and Ilana Blum, *Defining Second Generation Open Source Intelligence (OSINT) for the Defense Enterprise*, Santa Monica, Calif.: RAND Corporation, RR-1964-OSD, 2018.

[27] Defense intelligence official, interview with the authors, July 2020.

[28] For more information, see Bradley Knopp, Sina Beaghley, Aaron Frank, Rebeca Orrie, and Michael Watson, *Defining the Roles, Responsibilities, and Functions for Data Science Within the Defense Intelligence Agency*, Santa Monica, Calif.: RAND Corporation, RR-1582-DIA, 2016.

develop an analytic data science career field and data science center to facilitate analysis. To build on current efforts, we recommend that DIA and other intelligence organizations develop analytic tradecraft and methodologies to identify best practices to validate, incorporate, and analyze open-source data related to human activity and movements in an area of active operations in support of all-source, holistic target system network development to consider civilian harm. Moreover, as using open sources of information becomes increasingly codified to support dynamic operations, the services, with the support of the Under Secretary of Defense for Intelligence and Security, should investigate the feasibility of creating a specific military occupation specialty for OSINT, similar to those for human intelligence, imagery intelligence, and signals intelligence analysts and collectors.

Finally, most intelligence support to civilian-harm mitigation is conducted in the planning stages of an operation or strike. This focus is reflected in military doctrine and manuals, as well as the direction to consult population density tables and LandScan data to provide a strategic assessment on civilian activities to guide targeting decisions. Post-operation damage assessments conducted by intelligence officials are placed in the context of whether the military objective was achieved or the weaponeering choice was effective. The final phase of damage assessments provides the opportunity to determine the "overall impact of the damage on an adversary target system relative to the targeting objectives established," and combat assessments include a collateral damage assessment.[29] However, as was illustrated in the Raqqa operation, doctrine and training do not focus on assessing the holistic impact of a military operation on the civilian population. We have two recommendations. First, we recommend that DoD incorporate civilian protection into its pre-operation estimates and post-operation assessments of the cumulative effect of targeting decisions. This holistic network assessment can leverage the current battle damage assessment analysis process but can consider factors relating to how civilians live and move within the environment.[30] This can additionally support the prioritization of reconstruction efforts and complement intelligence tradecraft and training improvements. Second, we recommend research into how such tools as population density tables and LandScan can be further leveraged to support civilian-harm mitigation, including whether these tools can be adapted to support high-frequency, dynamic targeting efforts. Although they already provide a powerful intelligence capability in the planning process, more research is required to determine the efficacy of such an adaptation.

DoD Must Take Several Steps to Improve Its Ability to Assess and Investigate Civilian Harm, Including Improving Collection and Analysis of Civilian Casualty Data, Simplifying Reporting Procedures and Making Them Consistent, and Establishing Criteria for When the Military Should Conduct Site Visits

The U.S. military must improve its data collection related to civilian casualties—including the storage of and access to operational data—in order to draw on accurate, up-to-date information when conducting civilian casualty assessments. As the U.S. military increasingly operates

---

[29] Joint Targeting School, "Joint Targeting School Student Guide," Dam Neck, Va., March 1, 2017. An adversary target system includes all the targets that are in a particular geographic area and are functionally related or a group of targets that are so related that their destruction will produce some particular effect desired by the attacker. See Joint Publication 3-60, 2018.

[30] On the battle damage assessment analysis process, see Chairman of the Joint Chiefs of Staff Instruction 3162.02, *Methodology for Combat Assessment*, Washington, D.C.: Joint Chiefs of Staff, March 8, 2019; and Joint Targeting School, 2017.

in joint and combined commands, there needs to be a single program that tracks and stores the data needed for civilian casualty assessments. For example, DoD is currently exploring a system that would consolidate strike log and civilian casualty data to enable more-accurate tracking and recording of incidents, but resources and staffing solutions are yet to be allocated to develop or deploy such a system. Collecting and storing better data on strikes and civilian casualties will provide the military with an accurate picture of strike activity that will set the stage for more-accurate assessments of civilian casualties. Moreover, improved data collection and knowledge management will improve the military's ability to go beyond simply tracking incidents and provide valuable trend analysis and other research in support of improved military planning and mission effectiveness. The ability to track civilian casualties is analogous to monitoring other operational data, such as friendly force casualties and the number of enemy forces captured or killed, and the military must be able to track these critical operational data.[31]

To make reviews more efficient, DoD should encourage combatant commands to simplify their reporting procedures and establish clear guidelines for what is expected in civilian casualty reporting. First, to make it easier for civilians and NGOs to report instances of civilian harm, we recommend that DoD offer easy-to-use platforms for submitting these reports. U.S. Africa Command has developed a web portal for this purpose that has been adapted for use on mobile phones.[32] We recommend that this platform be extended across combatant commands. However, as discussed in the report, many victims of civilian harm were not aware that they could submit such information at all. To ensure that people use these systems, combatant commands should design programs and engage with embassy personnel to build awareness of the outlets among local and international NGOs working on civilian-harm reporting. One positive recent step in the direction of transparency and NGO engagement is the release of exact locational data for civilian casualty incidents assessed as credible by CJTF-OIR. This release will help those who are investigating and preparing civilian casualty claims better understand how the U.S. military records information about its strikes.[33] In addition, we recommend that all civilian casualty cells continue the best practice of canvassing traditional and social media for reports of potential civilian casualties, which then can be corroborated with operational and other classified information. This proactive step will reaffirm DoD's commitment to addressing civilian casualty reports in a timely manner.

Second, we recommend that DoD work to make civilian casualty reporting and assessment processes more uniform. Doing so would help civilian casualty cells assess potential civilian casualties more efficiently, reducing the amount of error or time spent asking for additional information or clarity. We recommend that DoD clarify what information these cells need to properly investigate a potential civilian casualty. For example, U.S. Africa Command's civilian casualty web portal requires the person filling out the report to note his or her "location of incident." But the form leaves a text box for open-ended entries and provides no guidance on the information expected. In the absence of any guidance for the user, U.S. Africa Command's civilian casualty cell is likely going to have a variety of responses that will take a lot of effort to make useful. Clearer guidance on what information is needed will reduce the amount of time that the cells report spending on information requests.

[31] Lewis, 2013.

[32] U.S. Africa Command, "Civilian Casualty Reporting," webpage, undated.

[33] For the location data for civilian casualty incidents assessed credible by CJTF-OIR, see Airwars, 2020.

Finally, DoD should establish clearer criteria for when the military should conduct site visits. One of the primary purposes for a site visit is to assess whether a U.S. military action was the cause of the reported civilian casualties. Determining this might require gathering forensic evidence to improve the military's understanding of the structure and mode of failure and of the terrain. For example, if the strike is estimated to have caused fewer civilian casualties than the casualty estimate (which is informed by CDE methodology), then the pre-strike proportionality assessment was likely valid. In such cases, no in-person visit may be required. However, if the number of civilian casualties may have significantly exceeded the casualty estimate, then the casualties have not been accounted for in CDE methodology, and there may be short and long-term lessons to learn from a more in-depth investigation. For example, in an investigation in Mosul in 2017 (also mentioned in Chapter Ten), the U.S. military learned that ISIS was deliberately staging attacks on the Iraqi Security Forces from structures occupied by noncombatants in order to draw coalition fire and inflict large numbers of civilian casualties. Coalition operations then adapted to account for this newly observed ISIS tactic.[34]

DoD Must Go Beyond the Identification of Lessons Regarding Civilian Harm—Exemplified in This Study but Also in Past Studies on Civilian Harm—and Ensure That They Are Acted On

DoD needs to strengthen its mechanisms for institutional learning to improve its ability to address observed deficiencies and not repeat past mistakes. As we examined the civilian-harm challenges in Raqqa, we realized that many of these challenges had been seen before in different contexts. In fact, no other country has such a rich history of assessments regarding civilian harm. These assessments include

- Multi-National Force – Iraq monitoring civilian harm in 2004–2006 to reduce checkpoint shootings[35]
- a series of more-comprehensive assessments for Afghanistan between 2009 and 2011, including the Joint Civilian Casualty Study, described as "the first comprehensive assessment on the subject of civilian protection"[36]
- a 2013 assessment for the Joint Staff Civilian Casualty Working Group identifying overarching lessons for institutional change as the working group came to an end[37]
- a 2018 Joint Staff assessment examining civilian harm in Iraq, Syria, and other U.S. theaters.[38]

The U.S. military has examined civilian harm more thoroughly than any other military has, offering a rich contextual understanding of why civilian harm tends to occur and the particular challenges that tend both to increase risk to civilians and to complicate the detection and accounting of civilian harm when it occurs. However, the robust set of recommendations available to DoD from these assessments often went unheeded; thus, many of the challenges

---

[34] General officer, interview with the authors, May 2020.

[35] Lewis, 2013.

[36] Sewall and Lewis, 2010, p. iii.

[37] Lewis, 2013.

[38] Joint Staff, 2018.

we observed were sadly familiar. Similarly, refinements to doctrine and training from operational best practices have been inconsistent at best. This lack of progress is likely a result of several factors: a lack of needed attention from DoD leadership, under-resourcing of efforts to clearly identify lessons, and unclear responsibilities for ensuring that institutional changes are made. For the military to adapt and improve over time, these responsibilities need to be clearly established, properly resourced, and sustained.

The United States can improve its ability to protect civilians by taking steps to strengthen institutional learning. Such steps can include the following:

- Establish an executive steering group that is led by the Office of the Under Secretary of Defense for Policy and includes senior representatives from the different services. This group can make overall commitments to actions to address civilian protection.
- Sponsor studies that examine lessons and opportunities from recent U.S. operations. For example, DoD and the services could maintain a program on civilian-harm studies that includes topics from recent operations.
- Hold conferences that bring together those with operational experience and those responsible for institutional change.
- Prioritize requirements for civilian protection capabilities by developing or improving both systems that specifically take into account risks to civilians (e.g., having icons for civilians or hospitals in a cockpit display, bomb defusing options, and strengthened tools for deconfliction) and systems that specifically reduce risks to civilians (e.g., using machine learning to help a system recognize Red Cross symbols, using artificial intelligence to strengthen CDE, and developing stronger systems for warnings and de-escalation).
- Use wargames to explore civilian protection considerations for future plans and capabilities. For example, the Office of the Secretary of Defense could promote the inclusion of civilian protection considerations in sponsored wargames and encourage the services to do the same.
- Leverage federally funded research and development centers' analytic agendas, which are a resource available to DoD but tend not to include civilian-harm issues.[39]

These steps would collectively serve to improve DoD's ability to identify and incorporate lessons and thus its ability to learn from past mistakes and challenges. Without a strengthened learning process, there is a real risk that the tragic circumstances seen in Raqqa will be repeated.

---

[39] Larry Lewis, "Recommendations for Strengthening Civilian Protection," Arlington, Va.: CNA, unpublished working paper, undated-b.

ANNEX

Geospatial Intelligence Analysis

The annex to this report is available for download at www.rand.org/t/RRA753-1.

Abbreviations

CCAR	CIVCAS credibility assessment report
CDE	collateral damage estimation
CENTCOM	U.S. Central Command
CIVCAS cell	civilian casualty cell
CJTF	combined joint task force
DIA	Defense Intelligence Agency
DoD	U.S. Department of Defense
ISIS	Islamic State of Iraq and Syria
ISR	intelligence, surveillance, and reconnaissance
JTAC	joint tactical air controller
NGO	nongovernmental organizations
OIR	Operation Inherent Resolve
OSINT	open-source intelligence
PAI	publicly available information
RFI	request for information
ROE	rules of engagement
SDF	Syrian Democratic Forces
SOF	special operations forces
SOJTF	special operations joint task force
TEA	target engagement authority
USAID	U.S. Agency for International Development
USMC	U.S. Marine Corps
YPG	Yekîneyên Parastina Gel (People's Protection Units)

References

Abdelaziz, Salma, Nick Paton Walsh, and Mohammad Eyad Kourdi, "Raqqa: Secret Video Shows ISIS Losing Chokehold on Its 'Capital,'" CNN, June 27. 2017.

Air Force Annex 3-60, *Targeting*, Washington, D.C.: Curtis E. LeMay Center for Doctrine Development and Education, March 15, 2019.

Air Force Instruction 51-401, *The Law of War*, Department of the Air Force, August 3, 2018.

Airwars, "U.S.-Led Coalition in Iraq & Syria: Airwars Assessment," incident CS1635, October 17, 2017. As of March 1, 2021:
https://airwars.org/civilian-casualties/cs1635-october-17-2017/

———, "The Credibles," web tool, last updated March 13, 2020. As of March 1, 2021:
https://airwars.org/conflict-data/the-credibles

Amnesty International, "War in Raqqa: Rhetoric Versus Reality," webpage, undated. As of March 1, 2021:
https://raqqa.amnesty.org

———, *Al-Raqqa Under Attack: Syrian Airforce Strikes Against Civilians*, London, 2015.

———, *"I Won't Forget This Carnage": Civilians Trapped in Battle for Raqqa – Syria,* London, 2017.

———, *"War of Annihilation": Devastating Toll on Civilians, Raqqa – Syria,* London, 2018.

"Amnesty International Says US-Led Coalition Destroyed Syria's Raqqa," France 24, May 6, 2018.

Anderson, D. J., and Jeff Davis, "Department of Defense Press Briefing by Brigadier General Anderson via Teleconference from Iraq," transcript, U.S. Department of Defense, July 6, 2017.

Athey, Philip, "New in 2020: More Gigantic Exercises for the Marine Corps," *Marine Corps Times,* January 21, 2020.

Ballard, John R., "Lessons Learned from Operation *AL FAJR*: The Liberation of Fallujah," 10th Annual Command and Control Research and Technology Symposium: The Future of C2, Washington, D.C., 2005.

Barnard, Anne, "U.S.-Backed Forces Begin Assault on Raqqa, ISIS Stronghold in Syria, " *New York Times,* June 6, 2017.

The Basic School, *Law of War/Introduction to Rules of Engagement B130936 Student Handout*, Camp Barrett, Va.: Marine Corps Training Command, undated. As of March 1, 2021:
https://www.trngcmd.marines.mil/Portals/207/Docs/TBS/B130936%20Law%20of%20War%20and%20Rules%20Of%20Engagement.pdf

Boer, Roos, Laurie Treffers, and Chris Woods, *Seeing Through the Rubble: The Civilian Impact of the Use of Explosive Weapons in the Fight Against ISIS*, Airwars and Pax, October 2020.

Brown, Charles Q., Jr., and Jeff Davis, "Department of Defense Press Briefing by Lt. Gen. Brown via Teleconference from Southwest Asia," transcript, U.S. Department of Defense, May 27, 2016.

Bureau of Counterterrorism, *Country Reports on Terrorism 2019*, Washington, D.C.: U.S. Department of State, June 2020.

Byman, Daniel, "The Intelligence War on Terrorism," *Intelligence and National Security*, Vol. 29, No. 6, 2014, pp. 837–863.

———, "US Counterterrorism Intelligence Cooperation with the Developing World and Its Limits," *Intelligence and National Security*, Vol. 32, No. 2, 2017, pp. 145–160.

Casagrande, Genevieve, "The Road to Ar-Raqqah: Background on the Syrian Democratic Forces," Institute for the Study of War Backgrounder, November 22, 2016.

CENTCOM—*See* U.S. Central Command.

Chairman of the Joint Chiefs of Staff Instruction 3160.01C, *No-Strike and Collateral Damage Estimation Methodology*, Washington, D.C.: Joint Chiefs of Staff, 2018, Not available to the general public.

Chairman of the Joint Chiefs of Staff Instruction 3162.02, *Methodology for Combat Assessment*, Washington, D.C.: Joint Chiefs of Staff, March 8, 2019.

Chairman of the Joint Chiefs of Staff Instruction 3370.01B, *Target Development Standards*, Washington, D.C.: Joint Chiefs of Staff, May 6, 2016, Not available to the general public.

CJTF-OIR—*See* Combined Joint Task Force – Operation Inherent Resolve.

Clausen, Christian, "Combat RPAs Integral in Defeating ISIS," 432nd Wing/432nd Air Expeditionary Wing Public Affairs, December 5, 2017.

Combined Joint Task Force – Operation Inherent Resolve, "Strike Releases," webpage, undated. As of March 1, 2021:
https://www.inherentresolve.mil/Releases/Strike-Releases/

———, "SDF Begins Raqqa Offensive, Progress Continues in Mosul," press release, June 6, 2017a.

———, "SDF Breaches Old City of Raqqa," news release, July 4, 2017b.

———, "CJTF-OIR Monthly Civilian Casualty Report," press release, October 27, 2017c.

———, *Combined Joint Task Force – Operation Inherent Resolve (CJTF-OIR) Policy for Reporting and Responding to Civilian Casualty Incidents*, Camp Arifjan, Kuwait, May 9, 2018.

Congressional Research Service, *Armed Conflict in Syria: Overview and U.S. Response*, RL33487, August 2017.

Cooper, Helene, "Revived After Mosul, Iraqi Forces Prepare to Battle ISIS in Tal Afar," *New York Times*, August 18, 2017.

Cooper, Helene, and Eric Schmitt, "Airstrikes by U.S. and Allies Hit ISIS Targets in Syria," *New York Times*, September 22, 2014.

Dalton, Melissa, Jenny McAvoy, Daniel Mahanty, Hijab Shah, Kelsey Hampton, and Julie Snyder, *The Protection of Civilians in U.S. Partnered Operations*, Washington, D.C.: Center for Strategic and International Studies, October 20, 2018.

Daniels, Jeff, "ISIS Fight Shows US Military Can Use Lower-Cost Weapons with Lethal Results," CNBC, July 19, 2017.

DeGhett, Torie Rose, "A New Kind of Bomb Is Being Used in Syria and It's a Humanitarian Nightmare," *Vice*, August 28, 2015.

Dillon, Ryan, "Department of Defense Press Briefing by Col. Dillon via Teleconference from Baghdad, Iraq," transcript, U.S. Department of Defense, June 1, 2017.

Dillon, Ryan, and Jeff Davis, "Department of Defense Press Briefing by Colonel Dillon via Teleconference from Baghdad, Iraq," transcript, U.S. Department of Defense, June 23, 2017.

Dillon, Ryan, and Eric J. Pahon, "Department of Defense Press Briefing by Colonel Dillon via Teleconference from Baghdad, Iraq," transcript, U.S. Department of Defense, September 7, 2017.

Dillon, Ryan, and Adrian Rankine-Galloway, "Department of Defense Press Briefing by Colonel Dillon via Teleconference from Baghdad, Iraq," transcript, U.S. Department of Defense, September 21, 2017.

Dillon, Ryan, and Adam Stump, "Department of Defense Press Briefing by Colonel Dillon via Teleconference from Baghdad, Iraq," transcript, U.S. Department of Defense, August 16, 2017.

DoD—*See* U.S. Department of Defense.

Dorrian, John, "Department of Defense Press Briefing by Col. Dorrian via Teleconference from Baghdad, Iraq," transcript, U.S. Department of Defense, April 12, 2017a.

———, "Department of Defense Press Briefing by Col. Dorrian via Teleconference from Baghdad, Iraq," transcript, April 26, 2017b.

———, "Department of Defense Press Briefing by Col. Dorrian via Teleconference from Baghdad, Iraq," transcript, U.S. Department of Defense, May 3, 2017c.

Executive Order 13732, "United States Policy on Pre- and Post-Strike Measures to Address Civilian Casualties in U.S. Operations Involving the Use of Force," White House, July 1, 2016.

Field Manual 6-27, *The Commander's Handbook on the Law of Land Warfare*, Washington, D.C.: Department of the Army and Department of the Navy, August 2019.

Field Manual 6-40, *Tactics, Techniques, and Procedures for the Field Artillery Manual Cannon Gunnery,* Washington, D.C.: U.S. Marine Corps, October 1999.

Foundation for Defense of Democracies and the Brookings Institution, "Economic Defeat of the Islamic State: Behind the Scenes of Operation Tidal Wave II," panel, May 10, 2019.

Fox, Amos C., "Precision Fires Hindered by Urban Jungle," Association of the United States Army, April 16, 2018.

Garamone, Jim, "Mattis, Dunford, McGurk Cite Coalition Progress to Annihilate ISIS," U.S. Department of Defense, May 19, 2017a.

———, "Defeat ISIS 'Annihilation' Campaign Accelerating, Mattis Says," U.S. Department of Defense, May 28, 2017b.

Garland, Chad, "A-10 Warthog Drops 2,000-Pound Bunker-Buster on ISIS Sniper Nest in Raqqa," *Stars and Stripes*, August 31, 2017.

George, Susannah, Qassim Abdul-Zahra, Maggie Michael, and Lori Hinnant, "Mosul Is a Graveyard: Final IS Battle Kills 9,000 Civilians," Associated Press, December 20, 2017.

Gibbons-Neff, Thomas, "Marine Unit in Syria Using Highly Advanced Artillery Ammunition, Video Shows," *Washington Post*, July 3, 2017.

Gibson, Daniel C., Scott Pence, and Stoney Grimes, "Smoke Employment in the Battle for Mosul," *Field Artillery Professional Bulletin*, No. 3, 2020, pp. 12–14.

Global Coalition Against Daesh, "Partners," webpage, undated. As of March 1, 2021: https://theglobalcoalition.org/en/partners/

Gordon, Michael R., "U.S. Is Sending 400 More Troops to Syria," *New York Times*, March 9, 2017a.

———, "U.S.-Backed Forces Close to Trapping ISIS Holdouts in Raqqa," *New York Times,* July 2, 2017b.

Gordon, Michael R., and Eric Schmitt, "Trump to Arm Syrian Kurds, Even as Turkey Strongly Objects," *New York Times*, May 9, 2017.

Haigler, Karl, "Guide to Intelligence Support for Military Operations," *The Intelligencer: Journal of U.S. Intelligence Studies*, Vol. 19, No. 1, Spring/Winter 2012, pp. 51–55.

Hall, Richard, "Raqqa Liberated from ISIS: 'My City Is Now Ruined and Burned Down,'" Public Radio International, October 19, 2017.

Al-Hamdan, Maher, "The Ongoing Medical Crisis in Raqqa," Atlantic Council, May 16, 2018.

Hassan, Hassan, "The Battle for Raqqa and the Challenges After Liberation," *CTC Sentinel*, Vol. 10, No. 6, June/July 2017, pp. 1–10.

Hebert, Adam J., "In Case You Missed It: Airpower Killed ISIS," *Air Force Magazine*, January 29, 2018.

Hendrix, Cullen S., and Wendy H. Wong, "When Is the Pen Truly Mighty? Regime Type and the Efficacy of Naming and Shaming in Curbing Human Rights Abuses," *British Journal of Political Science*, Vol. 43, No. 3, July 2013, pp. 651–672.

Hlad, Jennifer, "Punching Above Their Weight," *Air Force Magazine*, November 21, 2017.

Human Rights Watch, *Syria's Use of Incendiary Weapons: Memorandum to Convention on Conventional Weapons Delegates*, New York, November 2013.

———, "Syria: Landmines Kill, Injure Hundreds in Raqqa," February 12, 2018.

Ibrahim, Mohammad Abdulssattar, and Mateo Nelson, "A 'Shift' in Strategy in Raqqa City amid Rising Civilian, Military Toll," *Syria Direct*, July 18, 2017a.

———, "Islamic State Pushes Back Against SDF Advances in Southern Raqqa City," *Syria Direct*, August 1, 2017b.

Innocenti, Cynthia, "Shaping the Information War: Military Information Combats Propaganda," U.S. Central Command, April 11, 2017.

Institute for the Study of War, "ISIS Sanctuary: August 8, 2014," map, August 4, 2015. As of April 23, 2021: http://www.understandingwar.org/backgrounder/isis-sanctuary-map-august-8-2014-0

"IS Conflict: Coalition Strikes on Raqqa 'Killed 1,600 Civilians,'" BBC News, April 25, 2019.

Isler, Matthew, "Department of Defense Press Briefing by Brig. Gen. Matthew Isler on Central Command's Targeting and Civilian Casualty Investigation Processes," transcript, U.S. Department of Defense October 25, 2017.

Jo, Hyeran, and Beth A. Simmons, "Can the International Criminal Court Deter Atrocity?" *International Organization*, Vol. 70, No. 3, Summer 2016, pp. 443–475.

Joint Chiefs of Staff, *Developing Today's Joint Officers for Tomorrow's Ways of War: The Joint Chiefs of Staff Vision and Guidance for Professional Military Education & Talent Management*, Washington, D.C., May 1, 2020a.

———, *DoD Dictionary of Military and Associated Terms*, Washington, D.C., June 2020b.

Joint Doctrine Note 4/13, *Culture and the Human Terrain*, London: U.K. Ministry of Defence, September 2013.

Joint Publication 2-01.3, *Joint Intelligence Preparation of the Operational Environment*, Washington, D.C.: Joint Chiefs of Staff, May 21, 2014.

Joint Publication 3-09, *Joint Fire Support*, Washington, D.C.: Joint Chiefs of Staff, April 10, 2019.

Joint Publication 3-60, *Joint Targeting*, Washington, D.C.: Joint Chiefs of Staff, January 31, 2013.

Joint Publication 3-60, *Joint Targeting*, Washington, D.C.: Joint Chiefs of Staff, September 28, 2018, Not available to the general public.

Joint Staff, *Civilian Casualty (CIVCAS) Review*, Washington, D.C., April 17, 2018. As of March 1, 2021: https://www.jcs.mil/Portals/36/Documents/Civilian%20Casualty%20Review%20Report%20Redacted.pdf

Joint Targeting School, "Joint Targeting School Student Guide," Dam Neck, Va., March 1, 2017.

Jones, Seth G., James Dobbins, Daniel Byman, Christopher S. Chivvis, Ben Connable, Jeffrey Martini, Eric Robinson, and Nathan Chandler, *Rolling Back the Islamic State*, Santa Monica, Calif.: RAND Corporation, RR-1912, 2017. As of October 26, 2020:
https://www.rand.org/pubs/research_reports/RR1912.html

Khan, Azmat, and Anand Gopal, "The Uncounted," *New York Times Magazine*, November 16, 2017.

Kilani, Feras, "Fall of Raqqa: IS Fighters Seeking a Deal to Move Safely out of the City," video, BBC News, October 13, 2017.

Kipp, Jacob, Lester Grau, Karl Prinslow, and Don Smith, "The Human Terrain System: A CORDS for the 21st Century," *Military Review*, September–October 2006, pp. 8–15.

Knopp, Bradley, Sina Beaghley, Aaron Frank, Rebeca Orrie, and Michael Watson, *Defining the Roles, Responsibilities, and Functions for Data Science Within the Defense Intelligence Agency*, Santa Monica, Calif.: RAND Corporation, RR-1582-DIA, 2016. As of March 1, 2021:
https://www.rand.org/pubs/research_reports/RR1582.html

Kogan, David R., *The Coalition Military Campaign to Defeat the Islamic State in Iraq and Syria 21 AUG 2016–05 SEP 2017: The Sky Dragon Dismantles the "Caliphate,"* Combined Joint Task Force – Operation Inherent Resolve, 2017.

Kolenda, Christopher D., Rachel Reid, Chris Rogers, and Marte Retzius, *The Strategic Costs of Civilian Harm: Applying Lessons from Afghanistan to Current and Future Conflicts*, New York: Open Society Foundations, June 2016.

Kreisman, Rachel, "Raqqa and the Oil Economy of ISIS," Atlantic Council, May 15, 2017.

Lacey, James, "Finally Getting Serious About Professional Military Education," *War on the Rocks*, May 18, 2020.

Lafta, R., V. Cetorelli, and G. Burnham, "Living in Mosul During the Time of ISIS and the Military Liberation: Results from a 40-Cluster Household Survey," *Conflict and Health*, Vol. 12, 2018, article 31.

Lamothe, Dan, "There Are Four Times as Many U.S. Troops in Syria as Previously Acknowledged by the Pentagon," *Washington Post,* December 6, 2017.

Lamothe, Dan, and Thomas Gibbons-Neff, "Marines Have Arrived in Syria to Fire Artillery in the Fight for Raqqa," *Washington Post*, March 8, 2017.

Lewis, Larry, "Improving Policy and Practice to Protect Civilians: A Lifecycle Approach," Arlington, Va.: CNA, unpublished working paper, undated-a.

———, "Recommendations for Strengthening Civilian Protection," Arlington, Va.: CNA, unpublished working paper, undated-b.

———, *Reducing and Mitigating Civilian Casualties: Enduring Lessons*, Washington, D.C.: Joint and Coalition Operational Analysis, April 12, 2013.

———, *Improving Lethal Action: Learning and Adapting in U.S. Counterterrorism Operations*, Arlington, Va.: CNA, September 2014.

———, *Promoting Civilian Protection During Security Assistance: Learning from Yemen*, Arlington, Va.: CNA, May 2019.

———, "Recommendations for Strengthening Civilian Protection," Arlington, Va.: CNA, unpublished working paper, October 2020.

Lewis, Larry, and Sarah Holewinski, "Changing of the Guard: Civilian Protection for an Evolving Military," *Prism*, Vol. 4, No. 2, 2013, pp. 57–66.

Lewis, Larry, Elizabeth Young, and Michael Messer, *Adaptive Learning for Afghanistan: Final Report*, Washington, D.C.: Joint and Coalition Operational Analysis, March 2011.

Loveluck, Louisa, "U.S.-Led Coalition Declares ISIS Forces Vanquished, Battle for Raqqa Over," *Washington Post*, October 20, 2017.

Lowcock, Mark, "Briefing to the Security Council on the Humanitarian Situation in Raqqa and Rukban," United Nations Office for the Coordination of Humanitarian Affairs, April 17, 2018.

Malsin, Jared, "Raqqa Is in Ruins, and ISIS in Retreat," *Time*, November 6, 2017.

Margolis, Gabriel, "The Lack of HUMINT: A Recurring Intelligence Problem," *Global Security Studies*, Vol. 4, No. 2, Spring 2013, pp. 43–60.

Matsumura, John, John Gordon IV, and Randall Steeb, *Defining an Approach for Future Close Air Support Capability*, Santa Monica, Calif.: RAND Corporation, RR-1233-A, 2017.

McCullough, Amy, and Brian W. Everstine, "Moody's Flying Tigers Wrap-Up Intense Deployment Fighting ISIS," *Air Force Magazine*, January 10, 2018.

McLaughlin, Elizabeth, "100 ISIS Fighters Surrender in Raqqa in Sign That Battle to Retake the Syrian City Could Be Winding Down," ABC News, October 14, 2017.

McNeill, Sophie, "Raqqa: Monitoring Groups Sound Alarm over Civilian Death Toll as Islamic State Fight Heats Up," Australian Broadcasting Corporation, June 27, 2017.

Meilinger, Phillip S., "Air Strategy Targeting for Effect," *Aerospace Power Journal*, Winter 1999, pp. 48–61.

Mendelsohn, Barak, "The Battle for Algeria: Explaining Fratricide Among Armed Nonstate Actors," *Studies in Conflict & Terrorism*, 2019, pp. 1–23.

Micallef, Joseph V., "Sitrep Raqqa: The Geopolitics of Eastern Syria," Military.com, June 26, 2017.

Mihaylov, Dimitar, "Cracks in the Crescent: The Looming Sectarian Clash Between Khilafah and Imamah," *Israel Journal of Foreign Affairs*, Vol. 9, No. 1, 2015, pp. 49–61.

Mitchell, Ellen, "Mattis: Trump Strategy Aims to 'Annihilate' ISIS," *The Hill*, May 19, 2017.

Mogelson, Luke, "America's Abandonment of Syria," *New Yorker*, April 20, 2020.

Murdock, Heather, "Syrian Authorities Find 5,000 Bodies in Raqqa Mass Graves," Voice of America, September 4, 2019.

Najjar, Ameen, "Damage Caused by the Syrian Civil War: What the Data Say," Towards Data Science, June 27, 2018.

Al Nofal, Walid, Mohammad Abdulssattar Ibrahim, and Mateo Nelson, "'1km' Remains for Syrian Democratic Forces to Completely Isolate Raqqa City," *Syria Direct*, June 22, 2017.

Oak Ridge National Laboratory, "LandScan Program Overview," presentation, June 2020a.

———, "Population Density Tables," presentation, June 2020b.

Oakford, Samuel, *Death in the City: High Levels of Civilian Harm in Modern Urban Warfare Resulting from Significant Explosive Weapons Use*, London: Airwars, May 2018.

Office of the General Counsel, U.S. Department of Defense, *Department of Defense Law of War Manual*, Washington, D.C.: U.S. Department of Defense, December 2016.

Office of the Under Secretary of Defense (Comptroller), *Department of Defense Budget Fiscal Year (FY) 2017: Request for Additional FY 2017 Appropriations—Overseas Contingency Operations (OCO), Counter-Islamic State of Iraq and Syria (ISIS) Train and Equip Fund (CTEF)*, Washington, D.C., March 2017.

Office of the United Nations High Commissioner for Refugees, "Iraq Situation: UNHCR Flash Update," Geneva, July 14, 2017.

People's Defense Units, "SDF Statement on the Raqqa Victory and the Future of the City," October 20, 2017.

Petkova, Mariya, "What Will Happen to Post-ISIL Raqqa," Al Jazeera, October 17, 2017.

Raqqa Is Being Slaughtered Silently, Facebook post, May 28, 2017. As of March 1, 2021: https://www.facebook.com/Raqqa.Sl/photos/a.780113668666553.1073741828.780110825333504/1565169346827644/?type=3&theater

Raqqah Study Group, *What the Battle for Raqqah Teaches the Force*, Fort George Meade, Md.: U.S. Army Asymmetric Warfare Group, March 13, 2018, Not available to the general public.

Rasmussen, Sune Engel, and Michael R. Gordon, "A Small U.S. Base Gets in Iran's Way—but Maybe Not for Long," *Wall Street Journal*, December 27, 2018.

REACH Initiative, "Ar-Raqqa City, Syria—Situation Overview VI," Geneva, October 13, 2017.

———, "Situation Overview: Area-Based Assessment of Ar-Raqqa City," Geneva, March 2018.

———, *Syrian Cities Damage Atlas—Eight Year Anniversary of the Syrian Civil War: Thematic Assessment of Satellite Identified Damage*, Geneva, March 16, 2019.

ReliefWeb, "Ar-Raqqa City, Syria—Situation Overview, 13 October 2017," webpage, October 13, 2017. As of March 1, 2021:
https://reliefweb.int/sites/reliefweb.int/files/resources/reach_syr_ar-raqqa_city_situation_overview_vi_13_october_2017.pdf

Revkin, Mara R., "When Terrorists Govern: Protecting Civilians in Conflicts with State-Building Armed Groups," *Harvard National Security Journal*, Vol. 9, 2018, pp. 100–145.

Roberts, Brian, and Rene Peter Hohmann, "The Systems of Secondary Cities: The Neglected Drivers of Urbanising Economies," Cities Alliance, CIVIS No. 7, 2014.

Robinson, Eric, Daniel Egel, Patrick B. Johnston, Sean Mann, Alexander D. Rothenberg, and David Stebbins, *When the Islamic State Comes to Town: The Economic Impact of Islamic State Governance in Iraq and Syria*, Santa Monica, Calif.: RAND Corporation, RR-1970-RC, 2017. As of March 1, 2021: https://www.rand.org/pubs/research_reports/RR1970.html

Rosenblatt, Nate, and David Kilcullen, *How Raqqa Became the Capital of ISIS: A Proxy Warfare Study*, Washington, D.C.: New America, July 25, 2019.

Schmitt, Eric, Helene Cooper, and Alissa J. Rubin, "Trump Orders State Dept. to Suspend Funds for Syria Recovery," *New York Times*, March 30, 2018.

SecDev Foundation, "ISIS Steps Up Information Control in Raqqa and Deir Ezzor," *Flash Notes*, Vol. 5, August 5, 2015.

Sewall, Sarah B., *Chasing Success: Air Force Efforts to Reduce Civilian Harm*, Maxwell Air Force Base, Ala.: Air Force University Press, 2016.

Sewall, Sarah, and Larry Lewis, *Reducing and Mitigating Civilian Casualties: Afghanistan and Beyond – Joint Civilian Casualty Study*, Washington, D.C.: Joint Center for Operational Analysis and U.S. Joint Forces Command, 2010, Not available to the general public.

Sherlock, Ruth, Lama Al-Arian, and Kamiran Sadoun, "'This Is Not Liberation': Life in the Rubble of Raqqa, Syria," NPR, October 26, 2018.

Sim, David, "Battle for Raqqa Photos: ISIS Confined to Hospital and Stadium, with Hostages and Snipers in Both," *International Business Times*, October 3, 2017.

Sims, Jennifer E., "Foreign Intelligence Liaison: Devils, Deals, and Details," *International Journal of Intelligence and CounterIntelligence*, Vol. 19, No. 2, 2006, pp. 195–217.

Snow, Shawn, "4,000 US Troops in Syria?" *Military Times*, October 31, 2017.

———, "Marine Artillery Barrage of Raqqa Was So Intense Two Howitzers Burned Out," *Marine Corps Times*, November 2, 2017.

SOJTF-OIR—*See* Special Operations Joint Task Force – Operation Inherent Resolve.

Solvang, Ole, and Nadim Houry, *All Feasible Precautions? Civilian Casualties in Anti-ISIS Coalition Airstrikes in Syria*, New York: Human Rights Watch, September 24, 2017.

Sommerville, Quentin, and Riam Dalati, "The City Fit for No-One: Inside the Ruined 'Capital' of the Islamic State Group," BBC News, September 27, 2017a.

———, "Raqqa's Dirty Secret," BBC News, November 13, 2017b.

Special Operations Joint Task Force – Operation Inherent Resolve, "Law of Armed Conflict, Ethics, and Human Rights," LOAC Plan of Instruction, undated.

Svendsen, Adam D. M., "Developing International Intelligence Liaison Against Islamic State: Approaching 'One for All and All for One'?" *International Journal of Intelligence and CounterIntelligence*, Vol. 29, No. 2, 2016, pp. 260–277.

"Syria War: UN Says It Is Ready to Go into Raqqa," BBC, October 18, 2017.

Syrian Observatory for Human Rights, "'Euphrates Wrath' Operation Forces Control About 35% of Al-Raqqah City's Area and Prepare for the Conclusive Battle," July 12, 2017.

———, "Raqqa City: General Security After ISIS," October 20, 2018.

Tomson, Chris, "ISIS Fully Encircled in Raqqa City After Latest Kurdish Advances," Al-Masdar News, June 24, 2017.

Townsend, Stephen, and Adrian Rankine-Galloway, "Department of Defense Press Briefing by General Townsend via Teleconference from Baghdad, Iraq," transcript, U.S. Department of Defense, August 31, 2017.

Trevithick, Joseph, "Marines 'Burned Out' Two Howitzer Barrels During the Raqqa Offensive," *The Drive*, November 3, 2017.

U.K. Ministry of Defence, "British Forces Air Strikes in Iraq and Syria: Monthly List," webpage, September 5, 2018a. As of March 1, 2021:
https://www.gov.uk/government/publications/british-forces-air-strikes-in-iraq-monthly-list

———, "RAF Air Strikes in Iraq and Syria: June 2017," September 5, 2018b.

United Nations, *Report of the Independent International Commission of Inquiry on the Syrian Arab Republic*, New York, A/HRC/39/65, August 9, 2018.

United Nations Assistance Mission in Afghanistan, *Afghanistan: Protection of Civilians in Armed Conflict—First Quarter Report: 1 January–31 March 2020*, Kabul, April 2020.

United Nations Institute for Training and Research, "Damage Density of Ar Raqqa, Ar Raqqa Governorate, Syria," map, Geneva, November 21, 2017.

United Nations Office for the Coordination of Humanitarian Affairs, "Syria Crisis: Northeast Syria Situation Report No. 16 (1–30 September 2017)," October 19, 2017

U.S. Africa Command, "Civilian Casualty Reporting," webpage, undated. As of April 23, 2021:
https://www.africom.mil/civilian-casualty-reporting

U.S. Agency for International Development, "On the Record Interview with USAID Administrator Mark Green and Commander of US Central Command Joseph Votel, Al-Raqqa Province, Syria," press release, January 22, 2018.

U.S. Air Forces Central, Combined Air Operations Center, "Airpower Summary," October 31, 2017.

"US-Backed Fighters Move into ISIS Stronghold Raqqa for the First Time," *The World*, June 6, 2017.

U.S. Central Command, *Civilian Casualty Policy*, Command Policy Letter No. 85, Tampa, Fla., September 1, 2016.

———, "Syrian Democratic Forces Liberate Raqqah," press release, No. 17-409, October 20, 2017.

U.S. Code, Title 50, Section 3038, Responsibilities of Secretary of Defense Pertaining to National Intelligence Program, 2014.

"US Commander Says Syrian Arab Coalition Is Now Majority Group Within SDF," *Rudaw*, March 3, 2017.

U.S. Department of Defense Directive 3115.18, *DoD Access to and Use of Publicly Available Information (PAI)*, Washington, D.C.: U.S. Department of Defense, August 20, 2020.

U.S. Department of Defense Instruction 3115.12, *Open Source Intelligence (OSINT)*, Washington, D.C.: U.S. Department of Defense, July 16, 2020.

Vanden Brook, Tom, "New Rules Allow More Civilian Casualties in Air War Against ISIL," *USA Today*, April 19, 2016.

Violations Documentation Center in Syria, "Civilian Casualties in Aleppo," web tool, undated.

Wareham, Mary, "Dispatches: Incendiary Weapons Pose Civilian Threat in Syria," Human Rights Watch, June 21, 2016.

al-Wasl, Zaman, "Free Euphrates: Breaking the Media Blackout in ISIS' Raqqa," *Syrian Observer*, May 15, 2017.

Wasser, Becca, Stacie L. Pettyjohn, Jeffrey Martini, Alexandra T. Evans, Karl P. Mueller, Nathaniel Edenfield, Gabrielle Tarini, Ryan Haberman, and Jalen Zeman, *The Air War Against the Islamic State: The Role of Airpower in Operation Inherent Resolve*, Santa Monica, Calif.: RAND Corporation, RR-A388-1, 2021. As of April 23, 2021:
https://www.rand.org/pubs/research_reports/RRA388-1.html

Watson, Ben, "Weapons of the Syrian War: Airpower (Syrian)," *Defense One*, July 19, 2016.

Will, George, "Avoiding Collateral Damage," *Press Telegram*, September 1, 2017. As of March 1, 2021:
https://www.presstelegram.com/2010/06/19/avoiding-collateral-damage/

Williams, Heather J., and Ilana Blum, *Defining Second Generation Open Source Intelligence (OSINT) for the Defense Enterprise*, Santa Monica, Calif.: RAND Corporation, RR-1964-OSD, 2018. As of March 1, 2021: https://www.rand.org/pubs/research_reports/RR1964.html

Wolf, Mackenzie, "Marine Corps Artillery Support Vital as the Fight for Raqqa Intensifies," *Military Times*, June 27, 2017.